T0209980

When a *Butterfly* Speaks 2...

Celebrating the Return of the Silent Messengers
111 True Stories of Mystical Monarch Moments Blending Science,
Spirituality and a Touch of Numerology

Barbara J. Hacking

BALBOA.PRESS
A DIVISION OF HAY HOUSE

Balboa Press books may be ordered through booksellers or by contacting:

Balboa Press
A Division of Hay House
1663 Liberty Drive
Bloomington, IN 47403
www.balboapress.com
1 (877) 407-4847

Interior Image Credit: Mark Hacking

Print information available on the last page.

ISBN: 978-1-9822-4254-1 (sc)
ISBN: 978-1-9822-4256-5 (hc)
ISBN: 978-1-9822-4255-8 (e)

Library of Congress Control Number: 2020902028

Balboa Press rev. date: 02/21/2020

Dedication

I dedicate this book to the memory of Dr. Lincoln Brower, who passed away July 17, 2018 at the age of 86. He was an entomologist who studied the Monarch Butterfly population for more than 6 decades. Although I never had the pleasure of meeting him, I admired his advocacy and dedication to creating awareness and taking action to preserve this magnificent insect and its migration.

Dr. Brower was instrumental in helping the Mexican government set up the Monarch sanctuaries in the 1980's which are crucial to the Monarchs' migration and survival. Imagine where the Monarchs would be today without his foresight, along with others, including the Mexican people, who worked diligently to protect these treasured beings and their habitat.

Photo Credit: Donald Davis

"We should care about Monarchs like we care about the Mona Lisa or the beauty of Mozart's music. To me, the monarch is a treasure like a great piece of art. We need to develop a cultural appreciation of wildlife that's equivalent to art and music."

Dr. Lincoln Brower, 2013, Sweet Briar Magazine

Acknowledgements

A huge thank you goes to my family! Mark, it just seems like yesterday when you found that chubby Monarch caterpillar on Blue Mountain, when we were newly married.

You shared your love of nature with me and it was contagious! Since that moment, we have journeyed together through these days called life and have had many exciting Monarch memories, especially with our children Ryan and Rachel.

Butterflies have touched our lives in so many ways, bringing us together as a family, as we witnessed the miraculous metamorphosis of a butterfly. We learned to respect nature and appreciate all the gifts it has to offer. What we respect and appreciate, we protect!

Thank you to the butterflies who keep presenting me with life lessons over and over again until I get them right! I can't imagine life without them in it…and I hope I never have to! They truly inspire me and I am grateful for the return of these silent messengers as these books were being written. These stories wouldn't exist without them.

Thank you to my students who enthusiastically responded to having Monarchs in the classroom and to Serenity who helps me continue to see life through the eyes of a child now that I have retired. I have learned so much from all of you!!

Thank you to John G. Powers who was our family's mentor when it comes to Monarchs and other butterflies. You were our internet before it existed. We appreciate you always being there to answer questions and your passion was contagious. When you share Monarch magic with someone else, you never know what the ripple effect will be. Thank you for sharing! It changed my family immensely and our lives are better for knowing you.

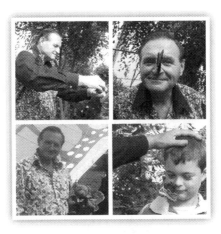

Thanks to Ev Scott for the reminders that I needed to write a book and modelling how to do that! Your continuous encouragement has meant a lot and I am grateful! Your grandchildren are blessed with Monarch Magic thanks to you.

Thanks to Dee Leifso for the equipment and push that I needed. I once gifted you with a butterfly and you gifted me with a journal which allowed my books to fly. I know why the Monarchs are following you.

Thank you to Mark Hacking and Angela Gerretsen who helped edit this book. I appreciate your precious time and skills so much!

Thank you to Pauline Bokkers for her ongoing support and teaching me so much about our bird friends. Nature is intricately connected. What we do to help one species, ultimately helps others too.

Thank you to Cathy Engelberger Kuczynski for the photo editing and the friendship that was created through the process. I will be eternally grateful for your kindness and the sharing of your incredible story.

Thank you to all the people who have come into my life and enhanced it, oh so greatly because of our mutual passion for butterflies. I have learned so much from each and every one of you and continue to do so. A special thank you goes to Mike Ward for helping me expand my knowledge of other butterfly species as well as pollinator plants. I love the way you help educate others about pollinators and gardening for them with your kind and gentle ways. The world needs more people like you.

Thank you to the people who have allowed me to share their amazing Butterfly stories. May they inspire others to believe in their magic. You have certainly inspired me with your courage and willingness to share. I have learned so much from you and you will always hold a special place in my heart.

Thank you to Ted Blowes, who was my mentor, for what retirement should look like. Unfortunately, he left this Earth far too soon, with work still left to be done. I shared my passion for butterflies with him and he helped me to realize this passion was a gift to treasure and share with the world. I know that Ted is still acting as a mentor and guiding many of my actions. The Ted Blowes Memorial Pollinator Peace Garden has become a very special and magical place for releasing butterflies and sharing Monarch magic.

Thank you to Luc Picard who became my inspirational guide on the magical Monarch mountains. You constantly remind me of the wisdom of the universe and how to surrender to it. You brought my attention to the special numbers that exist to give us much needed messages.

I am grateful to my wise parents who taught me the importance of family and to follow my passion. My Dad, Sylvester Eccles, a high school guidance counsellor by day, a gardener and poet during his free time and to my Mom, Dorothy (Campbell) Eccles, a primary school teacher, who baked the very best banana muffins and was the master of practical wisdom. They were such great role models of how to live a simple, happy life. How lucky I was to be their daughter! Not to mention that they gave me some really nice big brothers too.

A huge thank you to every person who has planted milkweed, gardened for pollinators, tagged Monarchs or cared about protecting our pollinators. Every action done by individuals can add up to a lot! We will never know how far the ripples of a single action can go.

I am grateful to Donald Davis who contributed his amazing photo of Dr. Lincoln Brower. Don holds the Guinness World record for the recovered tagged Monarch that traveled the furthest distance. He has devoted many hours to tagging Monarchs over the years and this gives scientists valuable information about migration patterns. He has also been instrumental sharing his vast knowledge with others.

Sara Dykman traveled 10,201 miles (over 16,000 km.) on her bike following the Monarch migration from the Mexican mountains up to Canada and then back down again. (2017) She was instrumental in educating others about the need to plant Milkweed (the only food source for Monarch caterpillars) and native nectar plants to help the Monarch population, as their numbers had dropped drastically in recent years. It was a pleasure to meet her before, during and after this miraculous journey. She inspires me in many ways.

I am grateful to Dr. Ellen Sharp and Joel Moreno Rojas for having the foresight to develop eco-tourism in the village of Macheros, Mexico and helping the visitors truly understand the plight of the Monarch butterflies in their overwintering grounds. To learn more about their valuable initiative, check out Butterflies and their People at www.jmbutterflybnb.com.

To the people who bought my first book, I appreciate your support, encouragement and positive feedback you gave me. It meant more to me than you will ever know.

Finally, thank you to the creator of all life. This truly is a magnificent world, filled with mystery, wonder and miracles. We just need to take the time to notice, enjoy and be grateful. Flowers and butterflies are just two of the many exquisite jewels of nature that everyone can afford.

Photo Credit: Mark Hacking

"Butterflies are self-propelled flowers."

R. H. Heinlein

Contents

The Monarchs are Leaving! Now What?

Choose Your Own Ending

Photo Credit: Nadia Martin

Teach the Children Well…
They are the Future

Introduction

July 18, 2018

It all started on January 31, 2017! It was the twelfth anniversary of my dear Dad's passing. I won a door prize which just happened to be a journal. Immediately the words mysteriously began to flow on to the paper and haven't stopped since. It's like a butterfly is sitting on my shoulder, whispering what it is I need to write and guiding me what to do.

For thirty years, I had the pleasure of teaching curious 6-8 year olds who were so eager to absorb all the knowledge they could. It was a privilege to be a part of their excitement for learning. Each Autumn, we bonded as a class by witnessing the miraculous metamorphosis that a Monarch butterfly goes through in its lifetime. It was a great way to get to know each other and transition into a new school year. Our first Open House was a time for the children to amaze their parents with astonishing facts about the magical Monarch. It was something that never grew old, and is still as exciting and fresh for me, as the first time I saw a Monarch emerge from its chrysalis as a child. As a teacher, I was privileged to be a part of each student's metamorphosis as they progressed through the school year and beyond.

When I retired from teaching in 2012, I had hoped to pass on this wonderful teaching tool. However, it was not to be! Teachers, who wanted to have Monarchs in their classroom and all the fun and learning they create, were asking for caterpillars, and I had nothing to give them. Mark, my husband, the biologist only found one caterpillar that September. If he can't find them, then they aren't there!

My retirement dream to witness the migration of the Monarchs at Point Pelee National Park was shattered. It is here that many of them gather before crossing the Great Lakes to the United States on their way to Mexico. Every September as a new school year began, I dreamed of the day I would have a chance to see this spectacular phenomenon. They weren't even doing a count that year, as there were too few Monarchs.

The Monarch population had reached an all time low in their overwintering grounds, on the mountains in Central Mexico, where they migrate to each November. The following year it was even lower. It was scary and sad at the same time. It was time for mankind to look at their actions and how they were affecting not only Monarch butterflies but many other animals as well; the pollinators in particular. **The Monarchs were speaking to us by their absence.** North Americans simply have to work towards the common goal of protecting these beautiful insects. Canada, the United States and México are all in this together.

> **"Some people talk to animals. Not many listen though.**
> **That's the problem." Winnie the Pooh**
> **(A. A. Milne)**

Milkweed, which is the only food source for Monarch larvae (caterpillars) was considered to be a noxious weed in many places along their migration route. Pesticides and herbicides used to eradicate it, are not kind to the Monarchs. Simply put, **without Milkweed, the Monarchs will vanish**. The province of Ontario, in Canada, took Milkweed off their noxious weed list in the spring of 2014, after recognizing that this was part of the problem.

I am happy to say that during the summer of 2017 and 2018, many more Monarchs have been observed here. The official count of the Monarchs in the overwintering grounds in Mexico revealed that the population was down 15 percent during the 2017-2018 season from the previous year. That was surprising after seeing more Monarchs that summer, at least in Ontario, Canada. This year, there have been even more and with optimism I am hoping that it will be a number much bigger than we have seen in recent years. Time will tell, as the count is usually done in December and announced in early March. Anything can happen as they migrate to Mexico.

Measures to ensure that the Oyamel Fir trees in their overwintering habitat are not cut down, were put into place by the Mexican government.

Reforestation projects have been helpful to ensure this valuable habitat is preserved for the future, as the Monarchs migrate here each November, to escape the cold weather in the north. We must keep in mind the Old Chinese Proverb, "The best time to plant a tree was 20 years ago; the next best time is now". Trees take time to grow, therefore it is not an instant cure.

When I visited Mexico in the year 2005 with the Monarch Teacher Network, many of the mountains were brown due to the trees being cut down. The people in the Mexican villages rely on wood for their cooking stoves and to generate an income. The canopy created by the trees gives them protection in the colder months and is essential for the Monarchs' survival. So there are conflicting needs. After visiting the overwintering grounds in Mexico in February, 2018, I am happy to say there was evidence of many young trees being planted.

At Cerro Pelon, one of the Monarch Butterfly Sanctuaries in Mexico, people have been hired to protect the Monarchs that overwinter there and their precious habitat. These much needed jobs help local families. The reality is that illegal logging often stems from poverty. Money to hire extra guardians to protect the Monarchs fully, comes from fundraising through an organization called "Butterflies and their People", spearheaded by Ellen Sharp and Joel Moreno Rojas. Illegal logging has decreased significantly since these extra people have been hired.

Climate change is another issue the Monarchs face. In March, 2016, much of the Monarch population was destroyed due to a rare storm of rain, ice and snow. Mark and I were visiting the Monarch Reserves in Mexico, just the week before, rejoicing at the sight of millions of Monarchs and experiencing beautiful sunny weather. While the Monarch reserves were hard hit with this unusual storm, up in Ontario we were experiencing beautiful early spring weather. It was as if we had shifted weather patterns.

Many of the trees in their precious habitat came down in that storm due to the fierce winds and heavy ice. Many of the Monarchs that had not yet started their migration north to Texas were killed. Monarchs are unable to fly when it is cold and roost on the trees snuggling together in order to keep warm. Their wet wings quickly froze. This act of nature, was devastating to the already dwindling Monarch population.

Texas is the place where they lay their eggs and die after spending the winter months in Mexico, leaving their offspring to continue the migration back up north. It is said that the great grandchildren of these overwintering Monarchs, are the ones we see back here in Canada.

How do they know where to go and when? How does a tiny little creature survive the journey? How does a wee egg no bigger than the head of a pin, transform into a beautiful butterfly? These are just some of the many mysteries of this amazing insect. What I love about Monarchs is that many of their secrets are just that! Secrets! Although well studied, they are still mysterious in many ways. The more we learn, the more we learn how much there is to learn or how much we wish we knew. Hopefully a tiny gps will be invented someday that will tell the whole story of their migration.

Yes, many of the secrets of the Monarchs remain, even in an age where smart phones do basically everything except go to the bathroom for us. That's what I love about them.

People noticed that there were very few Monarchs in their world and began to wonder why. Planting milkweed in gardens has become a simple way to help the Monarch and other pollinators as well. (bees, other species of butterflies and hummingbirds enjoy the nectar of milkweed's beautifully scented flowers) Planting native nectar plants is just as important as the milkweed. Once they are butterflies, Monarchs require nectar for nourishment. They can get this from many pollinator-friendly plants.

We don't want to only see butterflies in a museum in the future. Our children, and their children deserve far better than that. Wouldn't it be a shame if mankind with its ingenious capabilities of creating amazing technology couldn't find a way to preserve the Monarch butterfly and its miraculous migration?

Through the years, Monarch butterflies have taught me so much. The lessons they present as they flutter about peacefully are immense. We as humans can learn a lot from them. It is these lessons and experiences that now flow onto the pages of this journal. It is the amazing people that I have been led to because of my butterfly passion, whose stories are told and I am grateful that they have so graciously shared them.

Just a few short years ago, these stories wouldn't have happened because without Monarchs, our lives just wouldn't be the same and my books wouldn't exist. I am grateful beyond measure that they are making a comeback, at least here in Ontario. This can change drastically from year to year so we need to keep on doing what is working and stop doing what is not.

October 27, 2018

When I began writing my first book "When a Butterfly Speaks... Whispered Life Lessons", Monarchs were considered to be a Species of Special Concern here in Canada. They were even contemplating putting them on the Endangered Species list. As these two books have been written, I am happy to say there has been a resurgence of the Eastern Monarch population. It has been awesome to see our Monarch friends thriving and I am hopeful that it will continue. The Western Monarch population is still in jeopardy and very worrisome.

A friend of mine suggested calling this book "When the Numbers Speak" as I started to see lots of double and triple, even quadruple numbers throughout the writing of this book. I am not saying they are anything more than coincidental, but I did see them a lot. At first I would check their meaning but after a while I just saw them as reminders to be grateful for this amazing world, smile and pay attention to what was happening. I have always called 11 and 111 angel numbers but now include many more in that category.

When I was editing, I began to see even more intriguing numbers hidden among the stories as I looked more carefully at the dates, the chapter numbers, etc.

I think my new saying has become, "You just can't make this up!"

For those of you who think I have made these scenarios up, I thank you in advance for believing my mind is creative enough to conjure up such stories.

"Open your heart and mind like the wings of a butterfly.
See then how high you can fly."
(Zeenat Aman)

1

The Never-ending Story Ends... and a New One Begins

July 18, 2018

Today was a very special day in many ways! I finally ended the never ending book yesterday. At 1:11 a.m. I pushed the button to send my manuscript to the publisher. I purposely chose that time as I discovered I had 111 stories and I had always considered 111 to be a special number. I wanted to send the book out into the world with the best possible intentions. I had finally finished editing my photos along with my manuscript. While I was double checking everything, there was a moth flying around the room I was working in. Mark, my biologist husband, mysteriously woke up, came in, gently caught it and put it outside. A few minutes later, another moth was doing acrobatic endeavours around the room. It spiraled around me as I worked on the computer. I found it odd that it was circling me rather than the ceiling light. I decided to video this aerial performance for a few moments and I wondered if this little guy perhaps had a message for me as he landed right beside me facing my direction. Usually butterflies are the ones that bring me silent messages, but being that late, they would be tucked in for the night.

I believe, that this little moth was rejoicing because I had finally finished the writing of my book, "When a Butterfly Speaks... Whispered Life Lessons". He was doing a happy dance around me. When I looked at the video in the morning to see whether or not I had been dreaming, I noticed I had recorded it at 12:22 a.m. Little did I know that multiple numbers would be an ongoing theme for the rest of the day and the number 2 would be the star of the show.

Barbara J. Hacking

After lunch, I had to do an errand in Shakespeare; a little town very close to Stratford, Ontario, Canada where I live. On the way there, I noticed an electronic sign that said, "1:22 22 (degrees C.)." The 4 twos in a row stood out to me for some reason.

As I drove out of town, I noticed a road sign that said Road 111. I had never noticed these triple numbers before and I had been driving this road for over thirty-five years!

When I got in my car to return home, my dashboard read "2:02 22 (degrees C.)" Mmmm!

When I returned to Stratford, I stopped to take a photo of the Road Sign that said 111 and noticed underneath a 999 and a 000 on the same sign. Now, these numbers really had my attention. It was as if a light switch had been turned on and I could now see these intriguing numbers.

I continued home and passed the electronic sign once again. This time it said 2:12 and 22 (degrees C.). Again I stopped to take a picture as it was really quite unbelievable! If I had stayed there for another 10 minutes, it would have been 2:22 and perhaps still 22 degrees, but that would have been me trying to manipulate the numbers. Later, I would find that I didn't need to do that. The numbers showed up very well on their own without any help from me.

When I got home, I needed to change the file names on the photos for my first book. I wasn't sure how to do that, so I Googled it. Up came a Youtube video, "Renaming Photos on an IPhone" and it was 2 minutes and 22 seconds long. Wow, is all I can say!

Before going to bed, I simply had to look up the meanings of 999 and 222. The numbers 111 kept coming up as I finished my first book. Now, 222 seemed to be coming up a lot. Could it be the universe's way of proclaiming that the time is right to move on to book number 2? There had been many attempts to end book one which had ended unsuccessfully until now.

According to Google, 999 means the completion of a part of your life: anything that has required nurturing and has come to its natural conclusion. Also, according to Willowsoul.com it means pay more attention to new beginnings than endings. 222 means that a new cycle in life is about to begin. I don't think the messages could be any clearer than that!

When I went upstairs to go to bed, it was 12:22! You just can't make this stuff up!

2

Julia's and Gail's Birthdays

July 18, 2018

Today was Julia's birthday! She would have been 35 years old. I had the pleasure of teaching her when she was in grade two. Julia fought a tough fight with Cystic Fibrosis and endured two double lung transplants, before she passed away 7 years ago. I had hoped one of my Monarch butterflies would be out to help celebrate and remember the life of this beautiful soul. One of the chrysalids, was darkening in colour, signaling that the butterfly inside would soon be free, but it wasn't meant to be. I was so disappointed. It was teasing me!

When I went over to my friend Pam's house, which happened to be right next door to Gail's, Julia's mother, I discovered that tomorrow was Gail's birthday.

Pam had discovered some chubby caterpillars on her milkweed plants and I went over to check them out. We ended up going out to buy some bug cages and Pam kindly gave one to Gail as an early birthday gift. Gail loves animals of all kinds, and this Monarch was no exception.

What made today extra special was that Emily, Julia's younger sister officially registered "The Julia Lyons Foundation". Its purpose is to support CF Canada and create a much needed mental health program for CF patients. I can't think of a better birthday gift for both Julia and her mother. (www.Julialyonsfoundation.org)

July 19, 2018

A beautiful summer day was waiting to be discovered as I woke up. I went to attend to my Monarchs hoping to find a butterfly, but still the transparent chrysalis showing the black, orange and white wings within, remained unchanged since yesterday. Monarch butterflies usually eclose in the morning so they have time for their wings to dry before finding a place to roost for the night. Nature knows what it is doing, and the butterfly would emerge when it was good and ready and not before. I remained optimistic that there would be a butterfly for Gail to release on her birthday. I asked Mark to please call me if and when the butterfly was out, as I was off to work.

Just before I went out the door I had this feeling to check once more. I was so happy to find that the Monarch had decided to make an appearance. Its wings were already pumped up and it was clinging to the empty chrysalis shell allowing its wings to dry. In my hustle and bustle to get ready for work I had missed its entry into the world.

When a Monarch first ecloses (that's a fancy name for emerging), its wings are very small and its abdomen looks like a balloon. That's because it is filled with a fluid that will pump up the wings within minutes of it entering the world. Every time I witness this miracle, I am in awe of the process. How did that big beautiful Monarch butterfly fit into that tiny chrysalis? Monarch magic! A chrysalis is just a well wrapped package waiting to reveal the surprise inside!

I quickly snapped a photo through the screened enclosure before leaving. As I walked along the serene Avon River, I witnessed several butterflies dancing in the morning sunlight. They were especially enjoying the fragrant and colourful pollinator gardens that people had planted for them. People's efforts to plant milkweed and other nectar plants, not only beautified their homes but were helping the pollinators immensely as well. Planting Milkweed also helps people connect to what's happening with the Monarch. Milkweed, or Milkflower as I prefer to call it, is the only food source for the Monarch larvae or caterpillars. Without it, Monarchs would surely be something you only see in a museum.

Barbara J. Hacking

I entered Cora Couture, the beautiful ladies' clothing shop where I work. This smiling lady came into the store and said, "Oh! You are here!." I only work one day a week, so we were obviously destined to see one another.

She looked familiar, but I couldn't place where I had seen her before. It turns out that we had met in February in Macheros, Mexico at the JM Butterfly Bed and Breakfast. (www.jmbutterflybandb.com)

She and her husband were spending the winter months traveling around Mexico and had come to majestic Macheros to witness the spectacular overwintering grounds of the Monarch butterfly. The entrance to Cerro Pelon Monarch sanctuary is located within a few minutes walking distance from the bed and breakfast and is the home to millions of Monarch butterflies from November until March each year. From there, you rely on the horses and their trusted owners to guide you up the rugged mountain to the Monarch heaven waiting at the mountain's summit. If you want to experience this life-changing trip be sure to contact Ellen and Joel who are knowledgeable and gracious hosts.

It was lovely to see Karen once again and learn that they were living in Goderich which is less than an hour away from me. Like the Monarchs, they are spending the summer here in Canada before heading off next fall to travel to warmer places, while we Canadians experience the ice and snow of winter. We hugged goodbye, as we were now kindred spirits connected by our Monarch experience on the magical Mexican mountain.

The store was very busy today until around 4:00 p.m. I picked up my phone and noticed that the photo I took of the butterfly this morning, had a caterpillar in a "J" right beside it signaling that it soon would be a chrysalis. "J" for Julia! Monarch caterpillars find a suitable place to hang upside down just before turning into the chrysalis stage of their amazing metamorphosis. They then split open to form the chrysalis, shedding their legs, black stripes and head cap, as they are no longer needed.

So the butterfly decided to come out on Gail's birthday, not Julia's! This picture would be perfect for Gail's birthday gift. It would serve as a reminder that our loved ones sometimes send us messages in mysterious ways, if we are open to them.

I ran across the street to the camera store to have the picture printed and saw the perfect frame with the perfect saying for Gail. "Best Mother Ever" Gail has always been there for her three children and raising two children with CF-related medical challenges has certainly not been easy at times. Gail continues to maintain a positive attitude about life and sees things with a sense of humour. She is grateful for everything and always looks for the good in a situation. I have learned so much from this family and have been blessed with their friendship for almost 30 years.

At 7:00, I picked up Gail and Pam, to take them and the butterfly to the Ted Blowes Memorial Pollinator Peace garden. We marveled at the beautiful Ice Ballet Milkweed, as well as all the other blooming nectar plants.

There was a single Monarch circling the garden and we admired its beauty as well. Every time I have visited this garden recently, I have seen a Monarch flying solo. I'm sure it enjoys the company we bring when we do releases here. I must admit, I often think perhaps Ted has something to do with it. Could it be him watching over his garden?

Gail walked around the garden to find the perfect place to release the Monarch. She chose a spot right in the middle of the gorgeous flowers.

The butterfly began to flutter its wings but was hesitant to leave Gail. I gently placed it on her heart. It began to walk ever so slowly up to Gail's chin as she looked down upon her. It was a female butterfly. It had thick black veins on its wings and did not have the two black dots on the lower wings that are characteristic of a male Monarch. The butterfly continued to walk upwards. As it approached Gail's lips, she gave it a wee butterfly kiss. What a beautiful moment! Gail laughed as the butterfly explored her nose. Butterflies have long skinny legs and their feet feel like velcro sticking to you. It continued upwards and crawled over Gail's glasses, as it prepared for take-off. The butterfly then returned Gail's kiss on the forehead and took off into the gorgeous setting Sun's direction. What a privilege and honour it was to witness this wonderful release; so unique and special.

After this release, we climbed to the top of the bridge and spent some time watching the exquisite clouds. We even saw a butterfly cloud, as we enjoyed this lovely summer evening and Mother Nature's sky performance.

Happy Birthday Julia and Gail!

October 28, 2018

Gail and I had a pleasant visit today and were reminiscing about old times. We got out the photos from her birthday butterfly release and were especially drawn to the cloud pictures. We laughed at the one that we thought looked like the Cat in the Hat. Julia would have chuckled at that one too. The other two amazed us. Do you see what we saw?

January 19, 2019 (1/19/19)

Today, Mark and I saw this above statue while visiting the Canary Islands. (Right). It reminded me of the cloud we saw after Gail's butterfly release for Julia. (Top left). A girl looking free, as she tilts her head back and allows the wind to blow through her long hair. The statue was erected in 1991. So many 9's and 1's today.

3

There is No Such Thing as a Silly Question!

July 20, 2018

I jokingly warn people raising a Monarch for the first time, that they will catch Monarch fever of which there is no cure.

Today, I received a question from a family raising 3 Monarch caterpillars. Their smallest caterpillar had stopped eating and had been in the same spot for a day and a half. To top it off there was a black blob at the end of its body. They wanted to know if they had done something wrong.

I had failed to tell them that a caterpillar will shed its skin five times before becoming a chrysalis. It was doing just that! A child needs bigger clothes as it grows; the caterpillar needs bigger skin.

They also were surprised to see the beautiful gold line and the dots on the chrysalis. I used to tell my students that I thought the fairies painted them when no one was looking because the gold magically appeared shortly after becoming a chrysalis. Again, the gold is one of the Monarch mysteries. Glimmering in the sunlight, chrysalids look like garden jewels, although they camouflage quite well in the wild and are not easy to find.

Photo credit: Brilliant Images

After raising Monarchs for over 35 years I still am learning new things. For instance, the word chrysalis comes from the Greek word, "chrysos", which means "gold".

4

Releasing Old Patterns

**"I've always loved butterflies, because they remind us
that it's never too late to transform ourselves."**

(Drew Barrymore)

July 21, 2018

Butterfly releases can be useful for many reasons. Andrea, a year ago, released 4 beautiful Monarchs, each representing a significant time in her life. She realizes that the greatest growth in our lives often comes from the darkest times.

> **"Perhaps the butterfly is proof that you can go through a great deal of darkness yet become something beautiful." Beau Taplin**

She also knows that sometimes we find ourselves falling into old patterns that don't always serve our highest good.

Today's release was focused on releasing those old patterns and moving on into the future, developing new ways of doing things and different ways of thinking.

It reminds me of the old saying by Henry Ford,

> **"If you always do what you've always done, you'll always get what you've always got."**

Andrea was ready to change those old thoughts and ways of doing things. A butterfly symbolizes those transformations, and doing it with beauty, ease and grace. Its chrysalis is beautiful on the outside masking the big changes going on within. Louise Hay's affirmations, practiced daily were helping Andrea along this road into her future, giving her the confidence that anything was possible.

Similar to last year's release, the weather did not look promising before we got to Ted's garden. It looked like rain was on its way. When we arrived, the Sun came out and stayed with us like a faithful companion until we were finished. It then returned to the party behind the clouds but we were grateful for its appearance. So was the butterfly, as it was ready to be free.

Andrea brought her faithful dog, Koda. I couldn't help but tell Andrea about a recent video I had watched of a butterfly release, with a dog watching. As soon as the lady opened the container to let it go in front of an excited audience, the dog jumped up and ate it, much to the dismay of those looking on. I must say that Koda witnessed the release with very good manners and there were no casualties in the making of this story.

Andrea opened the lid as Koda watched. She gently coaxed the male butterfly onto her finger. She admired its exquisite markings, and then placed it on Koda. I don't think the butterfly liked the feeling of Koda's fur because as soon as he touched it, he sprung up into the air.

We sat down on the bench and there lying on the ground was a feather. We had been there for quite some time, and neither of us had noticed it. Andrea picked it up to remind her of this amazing release. This was not the first feather she had received recently. She found one on the floor in the library and the other one she found, mysteriously disappeared as quickly as it had come, although she had put it in a safe spot.

"Without change, there would be no butterflies."

Jayda Skidmore

Andrea decided that she would like to adopt a Monarch caterpillar so she could witness the amazing transformation they go through. We decided to go to my house to find her one. On the way there, the numbers 1 and 4 kept popping up. The time was 11:44 and everywhere I looked those numbers jumped out at me. I found it strange.

When we arrived at my place in separate cars I shared this with Andrea and she enlightened me that there was usually a message behind recurring numbers. All I had to do was Google it.

It's a good thing that I remembered to tell her about shedding their skin five times as "Henry" did exactly that, shortly after she received it. I think Andrea has caught Monarch fever! She will have company, as they transform together.

As I wrote this story and arranged Andrea's release pictures I noticed that the image number was 4411. How can this possibly be? When I Googled it, many meanings came up but the one that stood out to me and came up on many sites was to look for new ways to do things. Andrea was doing just that! Perhaps there is something hidden in these numbers after all.

Andrea's release is a reminder how our human life is similar in many ways to the metamorphosis of the butterfly.

We start life as a tiny being and we continuously grow in mind and body. Sometimes life presents us with events where we must transform in order to persevere, to grow and to gain strength. Often this takes time and patience. Strength comes as a gift from the struggles we face. Soon we are able to break out of the confines of the chrysalis we found ourselves in, which once protected us from the world around us. We are then free to fly

The butterfly reminds us how far we have come, how greatly we have transformed, how strong we have become in the process and how far we can fly. The sky's the limit!

5

Chrysalis Rescue

July 22, 2018

As I cleaned out the Monarch enclosure, I was lucky to catch the transition of a caterpillar into a chrysalis. Once the caterpillar is hanging upside down in a J-shape, it is just a matter of time before splitting open and revealing the chrysalis within. It wiggles as it does a "pupa dance" and releases its legs, black stripes, antennae and head cap. Shortly thereafter, it has transformed into an entirely different form. It happens quickly! If you turn your back, even for a short while, it is easy to miss.

Just before I was about to go to Ted's garden, to release today's butterfly that had eclosed in the morning, I received a text from my friend, Kelley. Her very first caterpillar had turned into its chrysalis, but it was sitting on the bottom of the container. I grabbed some dental floss and went to see what could be done. I lassoed the cremaster which is the black stick-like part at the top of the chrysalis and was able to hang the chrysalis up again. When the butterfly comes out, it has to cling to the chrysalis shell until its wings are pumped up and dry, without any interference whatsoever. Otherwise, the wings may not develop properly. Time will tell if this rescue attempt was successful.

Kelley and her husband, Daniel visited Macheros, Mexico last year with Rachel, my daughter, and I. We were able to experience the Monarch reserves together and saw millions flying around peacefully. They had captured Monarch Fever on those mountains!

I happened to bring my Monarch with me to Kelley's and it was ready to go as it had rained all day! I invited Kelley to release her first Monarch! She had experienced the Monarchs on the mountains but had never held one in her hands. She was worried that she would hurt it, but discovered that she didn't. A Monarch is much stronger than it looks, and if handled properly is just fine. It flew off across the road and then boomeranged back over Kelley's beautiful pollinator garden coming to rest on her roof. I always find it amazing to see how well they fly when they have never done it before!

Barbara J. Hacking

Author's Note: I had heard that if you leave a fallen chrysalis lying on its side, the butterfly will climb out unharmed as long as it can climb up somewhere to hang. I had a chrysalis without a cremaster, so tried this method. I am happy to say it was successful. I had it in a mesh container and it was able to climb up to hang and its wings were perfect.

September 7, 2019

Today Kelley left this world after valiantly fighting cancer for 20 years. Her family and friends will miss her strength, courage and determination wrapped up in her kind gestures for others. She seized every moment and made every day an adventure and she taught us to not wait to do those things on your bucket list.

At 10:30 this morning, her good friend Elena released a butterfly while her friends sent their love and prayers to Kelley and her family.

I had heard the news of her passing this afternoon and when I returned home there were 19 exquisite Monarchs out for Kelley. A beautiful reminder of Kelley and Daniel on the magical Monarch mountains in Mexico. Kelley is now free to fly like the butterflies she grew to love.

Butterflies represent transformation, freedom, beauty and happiness; all of which remind us of Kelley and the grace she brought to this world.

September 20, 2019

I was preparing the seven Monarchs that had eclosed this morning to take to Kelley's Celebration of Life. I carefully put one in each box and started to label them with words describing Kelley as she lived her life.

The first word that came to mind was Kind. Kelley was always thinking of ways to help those around her. Often she would host a coffee morning for her friends complete with freshly baked goods. She was always experimenting with recipes and the recipients were delighted.

Energetic, Living life to the fullest, Loving life, Happy and Courageous were words that quickly appeared. I realized that the first four letters of her name appeared with the first four words. I quickly added Exuberant and Young to represent her whole name.

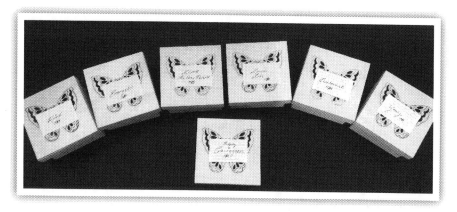

Kelley was too busy living to think about dying. Her amazing attitude and gracious spirit kept her going right up until the end. Those who knew her had been blessed having had Kelley in their lives.

6

Transformation From a Caterpillar Into a Chrysalis

"There is nothing in a caterpillar that tells you it's going to be a butterfly." (T. Buckminster Fuller)

July 23, 2018

I had been "cat" sitting for the Ford family who had gone camping for the weekend. The three children had three caterpillars. One had transformed into a chrysalis already and the other two were happily munching away on milkweed, or so I thought. Actually, I discovered one was missing. Thinking that the kids would be devastated, I put another caterpillar in the container. Upon their return, they were surprised that there were three as one had escaped before they left for camping. These caterpillars are small, but can travel quite far, very quickly and are excellent escape artists.

As the caterpillars grow, they require more milkweed. The more they eat, the more they excrete; and the bigger the caterpillar, the bigger the frass (which is a fancy name for poop). Can you find 6 caterpillars in this photo? Two are very tiny.

When the caterpillar is ready to make its chrysalis, it no longer requires milkweed. It will go on a walkabout, often off the plant it was eating to find a suitable spot. It then begins to create a silky white thread that will secure it to the well-chosen camouflaged place.

Once its lifeline is complete, the caterpillar will hang upside down in a "J" shape. That is the clue they will soon make the transformation into a chrysalis.

If you are lucky, you may see this process. Its stripes which are normally yellow, white and black, all of a sudden take on a greenish tinge. Between the antennae you can see a split in the skin. Like a zipper, it moves up the caterpillar's body revealing the chrysalis inside.

It no longer requires its black antennae, legs and stripes. The caterpillar does what is called a "pupa dance". It looks as if it is doing the hula. This helps free the black pieces and eventually they drop to the ground.

The "pupa dance" continues as the parts that remain become shorter and rounder. It takes about ten minutes until the new chrysalis is recognizable. Eventually, you will see a gold stripe and some dots develop.

The chrysalis stage lasts between ten and fourteen days.

Just remember if you want to raise a caterpillar, make sure you can take it with you if you go on holidays or know of a suitable "cat" sitter who can identify milkweed and know where to get it.

7

Serenity's Story - A Butterfly Coincidence

July 23 2018
By Serenity Sebben, age 8

My sheep, Brian, had to be put down today although I loved him very much. His sister died when they were just babies and I miss her. I was so sad that they both were gone that I cried under a chair with their picture.

After I went outside to feed the dogs, I went to look at the animals. I saw two Swallowtail butterflies. One was a boy just like Brian. The other was a girl like his sister. They were dancing in the pen over the other animals happily and it reminded me that they were together again. Then they both came down and landed on my head. They crawled down my face and gave me butterfly kisses like they were saying goodbye. Then they flew away and came back. They landed right in the center of my palm and tickled me. I knew they were okay.

Then that night I went to my Auntie Barb's. I remembered that they were gone. At bedtime, I cried with her right there beside me.

She said, "Just remember that they're in a better place now and they are watching over you. They do not want you to be sad."

I said, "I am sad, but I know that they are happy. Now I know that they are okay, I'm okay too."

The next day we went to the butterfly garden. There we saw a Monarch butterfly and it was a boy.

When we got back a butterfly had come out of a chrysalis. Then we let it go for Brian..

Author's Note: After the butterfly release for Brian, we saw a double rainbow while driving in the car. It was so beautiful! We got out of the car and just stood there in awe. We weren't surprised when a Monarch flew past us and then took off under the rainbow. Perhaps it was the butterfly, Serenity released for Brian. We will never know.

Serenity chose the title of this story and these are her words exactly with only spelling and punctuation corrections and a few minor edits.

8

Moths vs. Butterflies

"Pleasure's a Moth, that sleeps by day and dances by false glare at night; but Joy's a Butterfly, that loves to spread its wings in Nature's light."

(W. H. Davies)

July 26, 2018

Make a silky cocoon whereas butterflies make a shiny chrysalis.

Open their wings when resting whereas butterflies rest with their wings closed.

Their antennae are short and feathery whereas butterflies have long, skinny antennae.

Have their meals at night whereas butterflies feed during the day.

So although they both belong to the Lepidoptera family and look very much alike, there are differences.

This beautiful moth was discovered one evening in Macheros, Mexico, right next to the Cerro Pelon Monarch Reserve. By putting up a white sheet on a wall at night with a black light you can attract these special pollinators and get a closer look. The patterns are exquisite and a perfect example of symmetry.

I often have little evening visits from moths. They come tapping at the window.

9

To Dine or Not to Dine
With a Chrysalis

July 27, 2018

Today was our daughter, Rachel's birthday and we were meeting her and her husband, Jeff for lunch to celebrate. Jeff's birthday was the week before so we presented them with two Monarch chrysalids. If timed correctly, they would emerge, to be released on their upcoming anniversary. Nature has total control over whether or not that happens.

The server approached our table and informed us that we had to take these presents outside. When asked why, she said that it was a health hazard. She probably assumed they were some creepy bugs. It was too hot to put them in the car. That's why we brought them in, in the first place.

So, I took the chrysalids out and put them under the restaurant's sign. Luckily, we had a window table and we were able to keep an eye on these precious items.

Now if the container had been full of caterpillars, I could see them being a risk in case one of them escaped. Finding a butterfly larvae in your food, may give you something to complain about... but...a chrysalis?

10

Cloud Artists

July 28, 2018

After I retired from teaching, I began to notice how beautiful clouds can be. I was so busy with my primary students that I don't think I ever looked up. I guess I was always looking down upon the children.

As I left Avon school for the last time as a staff member, I circulated around the school's pollinator garden. I was led by a Monarch butterfly who had awaited my departure from the school. I think she purposefully flew upwards, drawing me to look towards the azure sky. I can remember discovering these miracles of nature, that I had ignored for so long, in the first few moments of my retirement.

Being a primary teacher, I was gifted with a great imagination. Now when I see white fluffy clouds, they put on a show in the sky. I often see butterflies and they make me smile.

Today, at our friend's' cottage, I was entertained by the clouds. I just love watching them dance before my eyes. Often they change quickly from one shape to another. Today's gentle breeze made that so. What do you see?

Once I showed my class a photo of a cloud that looked like an angel. When I asked the students what they thought it was, there were as many different answers as there were children. It shows that imagination is just that! A cloud can be anything you want it to be and others may perceive it entirely in a different way.

> **"The moment one gives attention to anything, even a blade of grass, it becomes a mysterious, awesome, indescribably magnificent world in itself."**
>
> **Henry Miller**

11

Towards the Light

July 30, 2018

My friend Sheila, texted me today that a butterfly was flying frantically in their skylight. It was as if it was stuck on the roof of their outdoor deck. It just kept flying upwards towards the light, banging into the glass, although the sides of the deck were open and it could go free at any time. In the process, it had damaged a lower wing. I quickly drove to her place and with a long net, we were able to coax it gently down before it hurt itself further.

I drove this beautiful Giant Swallowtail to Ted's garden and released it on one of the pollinator plants. It immediately began to nectar with its straw-like proboscis. It was so hungry and exhausted after its episode under the skylight.

I saw another Giant Swallowtail circle the garden, so I knew it would be in good company. It was still able to fly so it was in the perfect spot for a butterfly; a pollinator garden filled with decadent nectar plants and a friend.

When we had escapees at school, the butterflies were never difficult to find, as they always seemed to fly towards the natural light coming in a window.

Last Autumn, Mark and I stopped at Port Bruce, Ontario, during the migration season. We would espy a Monarch flying along the shoreline towards us and then it was gone. It seemed like they were flying one by one down the beach and then they would vanish into thin air. It had to be an optical illusion as butterflies don't just disappear. Mark and I both had our cameras ready and became perplexed.

Upon further investigation, we discovered that as soon as a butterfly reached a certain spot on the beach it would head out over the water; directly into the sunlight. It was spectacular to watch. Each Monarch came from the same direction down the beach and then turned at the exact same spot as the previous one to go out over the sparkling water. They definitely knew where they were going! It was as if they were playing Follow-the-Leader.

When looking at a map, one would guess that they were crossing Lake Erie and entering the United States on their way to Mexico. The key word is "guess". It was a perfect day for flying and we felt as though we had hit the jackpot, arriving there at just the right moment. Mother Nature works in such miraculous ways!

Barbara J. Hacking

August 1, 2018

Light seems to be a very important factor when it comes to Monarchs migrating. The shorter days as well as the cooler temperatures signal them to get moving. Regardless, the Monarchs that eclose in the late Summer and early Autumn will be very different than the ones fluttering about the gardens all Summer nectaring and reproducing. They are larger, can fly farther but are not able to reproduce at this time. They also have a lifespan 8 times longer.

Amazingly, these Super Generation Monarchs will travel many thousands of miles/kilometres to escape the colder weather. When I used to release Monarchs with my students in the Fall, they always flew in the same direction. How do they know which way they must go to get to Mexico? There are no parents teaching them. There is no instruction manual. Monarch migration is so intriguing.

The Monarchs east of the Rocky Mountains will end up on the mountains in Central Mexico, whereas those west of the Rockies engage in a Californian migration. How do they know exactly where to go year after year never being there before?

When the temperature is cool/cold, the Monarchs huddle together for warmth on the trees located at the summits of these mountains. When the Sun shines and it is warm enough, the Monarchs will burst off of the trees into a spectacular display of air ballet. They dance gracefully, never colliding within the kaleidoscope of flying friends.

In mid February or early March the Monarchs will then begin reproducing and the females will carry the eggs up to Texas. There they will find milkweed to lay their precious gifts on. They will then die and the new generation will continue to migrate North as the milkweed pops up. It is said that it is their grandchildren and great grandchildren that return to Canada in the late Spring.

August 2, 2018

Today, I was reminded how important sunlight is to the Monarch emerging from its chrysalis. Yesterday, was a dull, cloudy day and I didn't have any Monarchs eclose. Today, is a perfectly sunny day and there are five ready to split open like a sizzling popcorn kernel, at any moment.

In thirty-five years of raising Monarchs I have rarely seen one emerge at night. It appears that they wait until the morning light has shone for a few hours before peeking out into the world. It gives them time to dry their wings and test them out before dark sets in once again. Nature is amazing and knows what it is doing!

When teaching with the Monarchs, they usually came out in the morning and were ready to be released at the end of the school day.

12

How Do You Count Monarchs?

July 31, 2018

A friend posted a beautiful photo of some Monarchs nectaring with the comment, "How many Monarchs do you see?" and tagged me. It reminded me of the amazing Monarch season we are having this year and had last year after many years of seeing very few.

I sent a photo I had taken at the El Rosario Monarch Sanctuary in Mexico, when I was there in February and kiddingly asked her the same question.

I was happy to see so many Monarchs in one place here in Canada. The Monarchs are back and people are noticing… and they are smiling… and they are sharing! (on social media).

The process of counting Monarchs has always puzzled me. How does one count butterflies?

An official count of the Monarch population in the Mexican overwintering grounds is released every year, usually in March. It is measured by the number of hectares (acres) of trees that are covered in Monarchs. Common sense tells me this is an estimate only as it really is impossible to count individual Monarchs, whether they are huddled together on the Oyamel fir trees or free-flying in the air. It reminds me of trying to guess how many jelly beans there are in a jar, only on a much larger scale.

It does however, alert us to the fact that in recent years the Monarch population was almost non-existent and man must look at their actions before it is too late.

How many Monarchs do you see?

My dream is to see the Monarch population return to its former glory. Wouldn't it be lovely to see the Magical Monarch mountains completely covered in an orange blanket? There would be so many that a count wouldn't be necessary; we would just know they were back!

We are seeing many Monarchs this summer, so this dream may come true in the near future.

What do you see here?

13

Hanging On For Dear Life!

August 2, 2018

I opened the door of our Monarch enclosure this morning and was greeted with five chrysalids ready to eclose. The orange and black wings could be seen peeking through the now transparent shell of each chrysalis. The Sun was shining profusely through the window so I knew it would be soon.

When I checked again a few minutes later I saw a newly eclosed Monarch fall to the ground. I immediately offered it my finger and allowed it to hang. Its abdomen was filled with a liquid which pumped into the tiny wings. They grew quickly and now had to dry. Any interference at this time could result in damaged wings.

The Monarchs have little claw-like features on the end of their feet which work like Velcro. This one hung onto my finger for dear life. It wasn't going to fall again!

When Monarchs eclose they are upside down. They quickly turn around and cling to the empty chrysalis shell. Very rarely do they fall. Luckily, I happened to be there at the right time.

Barbara J. Hacking

For the first time since beginning to raise Monarchs, I noticed that the black line at the top of the chrysalis has a purpose. The butterfly breaks the chrysalis open at the bottom exactly in the middle of that line. When it turns right side up to allow its wings to grow and dry, it clasps on the outer edges of this line. It must be there to provide structure so the empty shell does not crumble during this very important part of the metamorphosis. Nature has been designed so perfectly.

December 1, 2018

Happy 50th Birthday, Kim!

My friend, Kimberly (Sunshine) Parry, The Butterfly Whisperer®, and her husband, Grant Slater, have their own beautiful story of "Hanging on For Dear Life". I apologized for having to put this story in the 13th chapter, but when I found out the date of their wedding, I just laughed and just knew it was meant to be here.

You see, Kim and Grant were married on August 13, 2016. Kim looked gorgeous wearing her custom gown adorned with over 500 fabric butterfly appliqués. Unfortunately, torrential rain during their outdoor reception meant that their wedding photos were not what they had hoped for. But, through much synchronicity, Kim's dream of having a unique "Butterfly Bride" picture taken to highlight her special dress did come true. She and Grant took a delayed honeymoon and drove all the way from Ontario, Canada to New Hampshire, USA to work with photographer, Jay Philbrick.

Hanging by a rope, the couple climbed 40 feet straight down a cliff to a ledge located 400 feet above the valley floor. Wanting to catch the beautiful sunrise in the background, they had to do this in the twilight of the new day dawning. The climb was a physical challenge for both of them. The exquisite photos were well worth it and they rose to the challenge beautifully. I guess you could even say they were lowered to the challenge.

Photo Credit: Jay Philbrick

Kim explained to me that being on the ledge was like standing at the edge of Heaven. After close to two hours of posing, Kim remembers wishing she had a live butterfly to release during such a spiritual experience. Just then a feather dislodged from her dress and started to float over the edge. She caught it and then ceremoniously released it in place of a butterfly. When the final photos were received, she was overjoyed to discover that this special moment had been captured.

Photo Credit: Jay Philbrick

14

Is my Butterfly Okay?

August 3, 2018

My friend messaged me today wondering if her Monarch that had just eclosed was okay. His wings had pumped up and then a reddish-brown liquid was expelled. She wondered if it was hurt or hungry.

I reassured her that it was perfectly normal and it was getting rid of what it no longer needed. It is the part of the caterpillar that is not required by the butterfly. This liquid is stored in the intestines until the butterfly emerges.

I had one excrete that liquid which is called meconium on my head yesterday when I was videotaping a Monarch eclosing. A first for me! Every day is different when sharing your life with the Monarchs.

Silly me! It happened again! I must learn to not put my head in the enclosure, especially when there are several Monarchs waiting for their wings to dry right above your head.

15

Shannon's Beauty Shines Through

August 3, 2018 (8/3/2018)

Yesterday I contacted my friend, Shannon, to see if she would like to release some Monarchs. We made a date to meet at the Ted Blowes Memorial Pollinator Peace Garden this morning at 9:00. When I checked the weather, it was calling for clouds, except at 9:00. Very promising for a wonderful release.

This morning when I got in my car, I saw 777 on the odometer. I quickly checked Google for the meaning of that triple number and was not surprised. It said that "something awe-inspiring and beautiful was about to happen"... and it did! (Willowsoul.com)

It was a morning dripping in perfection. Shannon and her sweet dog, arrived at the garden as the sun shone down smiling on what was about to take place. Five Monarch butterflies were awaiting their freedom, just like Shannon, who was awaiting her freedom from breast cancer.

From the first moment I met Shannon, I was impressed with her beautiful smile, her positive attitude and her amazing ability to lift the spirit of others with her kind words. Even with her diagnosis and treatments she continues to grace this Earth with her bubbly personality and a twinkle in her eyes. Shannon has always been a giver and it was now time for her to receive.

Shannon was intrigued with the Monarchs and was eager to set them free. The first one took off into the air as soon as she lifted the lid.

The second Monarch was launched off of Benji. As soon as the butterfly's feet touched his fur, it was off in a hurry. The third and fourth were gone in a flash too.

This release was going very quickly and it was now time for the final Monarch. It must have sensed our hope that it would stick around for a bit. Shannon decided to do the final release near a beautiful planting of Echinacea. She carefully took the butterfly out of the container and placed it on the flower. The Monarch was content to sit for a bit while we admired its beauty. Finally, it too was off into the air.

I often look for interesting clouds after a release. We did see one that looked like a trumpet vine or a lily. Later when looking at the photos, I noticed the sun looked like a heart peeking through the trees. Perhaps it was sending Shannon its love, as we all are, as Shannon fights this cruel and life-changing disease.

Shannon continues to inspire others with her strength, her grace and her commitment to remain positive. She teaches others how to live life to the fullest with her fine example. It truly was an awe-inspiring morning and Shannon's beauty shone through with flying colours.

Today's date is full of angel numbers. The month and day add up to 11 and the numbers in 2018 add up to 11.

Barbara J. Hacking

October 10, 2018

Yesterday Shannon got to ring the gong at the hospital. This is a tradition when a patient is finished their last chemotherapy treatment.

Today Shannon released three little Yellow Sulphur butterflies to celebrate. It was delightful sitting in the garden, watching the many butterflies and bees dancing from flower to flower sipping on the nectar. There were no Monarchs! Hopefully they are taking advantage of this fine weather to travel south.

The sunshine was smiling and so was Shannon. Little Cullen joined in the celebration too. He was at the garden with his Dad enjoying this fine Autumn day.

16

Garden Gratitude

August 4, 2018

I woke up early this morning filled with gratitude for Ted's garden, officially called The Ted Blowes Memorial Pollinator Peace Garden. I talked extensively about its creation in my first book, so today I will focus on how this garden has metamorphosed over the past year. I am beginning to realize just how important this garden has become in my life.

Every time I have visited this magical place this summer, I have seen a Monarch circling the four wings of its butterfly shape. I am reminded of Ted and what he stood for. He was a teacher, an environmentalist, and a mentor for all who want to make this world a better place.

For some reason, I was just drawn to look at my golden journal that houses the "Tribute to Ted" I wrote for the opening of his garden. I don't know why, but nothing surprises me anymore. I just listen to the words that circulate within me. When I picked the journal up, out dropped the order of the ceremony.

> Ted Blowes Memorial Pollinator Peace Garden
> Dedication Ceremony
> July 20, 2017

A year ago, I wasn't aware of "Angel Numbers" and their meanings. I am now just beginning to notice double and triple numbers and when I Google them I am amazed at the messages they deliver.

I Googled 2020, which I saw immediately when I looked at the date at the top of the program. Wow!

"Angel Number 2020 encourages you to display compassion, diplomacy, consideration and adaptability as you passionately serve others in your day to day life."
(Sacredscribesangelnumbers.blogspot.com, Joanne Walmsley, March 3, 2015, Angel Number 2020)

That describes Ted exactly. He lived his life to serve his community and did it very humbly with great enthusiasm. In fact, the saying, "So Proud To Serve, So Pleased To Assist" was printed on the front of the little brochure passed out at his "Celebration of Life".

Ted's garden continues his legacy. It teaches. It helps the pollinators by giving them habitat and it brings calm to our stressful lives. It reminds us to enjoy the peace in our lives that many gave their lives for and never take it for granted.

The nectar-rich flowers have grown and filled in the garden so beautifully.

Many pollinators have found refuge here from the chemicals man uses to control the environment and the ever-expanding urbanization of the land which robs them of their homes. People visit each day from far and near, enjoying its beauty and the lessons it teaches.

Many of the baby Ice Ballet Milkweed plants growing here from last Fall's harvest of seeds, have gone out into people's gardens to expand what this garden is already doing. Many of those plants already were adorned with Monarch eggs and babies. With time and awareness, hopefully we will give back what mankind has taken from them.

The garden never disappoints when butterfly releases take place here. The nearby waterfall and the songs of the birds serenade from a distance. The Sun shines, casting its glow on the rainbow of delicately scented flowers. The fluffy white clouds dance against the baby blue sky above this pollinator paradise creating an enchanting experience. I am grateful for

Mother Nature and all she has to offer; if only we take the time to notice her intricate handiwork.

Even the cicadas came out of their 17 year burial to molt and mate. They were enjoying Ted's garden too.

"The earth laughs in flowers."

Ralph Waldo Emerson

November 4, 2018

Today I woke up to an email which saddened me immensely. One of the concrete benches at Ted's Garden had been carried to the top of the bridge and dropped. It smashed all over the place. It would have taken quite a few people to do that!

With every bad situation comes something good. Serenity, 9 years old and her brother Tristan, 10 years old, decided they were going to raise money for a new bench after there was a public outcry on social media. Serenity made bracelets and Tristan offered his services to do odd jobs for people. Within 24 hours they had enough for almost 2 benches. These children had released butterflies here in the summer and they love this garden too! I am grateful for their kind hearts and their ability to turn around an otherwise horrible occurrence.

I love this quote.

"We can be unhappy about many things, but joy can still be there...

It is important to become aware that at every moment of our life, we have the opportunity to choose joy... It is in the choice that our true freedom lies and that freedom is, in the final analysis, the freedom to love."

Henri J.M. Nouwen

17

Oh Henry

August 4, 2018

Yesterday, I received a text from my friend, Andrea, that her butterfly had eclosed and she was pretty sure it was a Henry and not a Henrietta.

Andrea was excited that she had had a chance to make changes in her life during the time Henry the caterpillar was in his chrysalis. As she released Henry, the butterfly, she was saddened to say goodbye, but was grateful that he was with her, as they transformed together. They were now ready to begin their new lives and were both free to fly.

Andrea also shared the transformation of Henry with her friends on Facebook. They were delighted to experience the miracle of the Monarch's metamorphosis vicariously through Andrea's experience.

Another friend, sent me a message saying that her 16 year old dog, also Henry, was ready to cross the rainbow bridge and would be doing so at 4:30. How could that be? It seemed like just yesterday, that Henry was a tiny ball of fur, charming everyone he came in contact with. Henry was much more than a dog to Pam. He was her loyal companion and they adored each other. Henry was even known to sing along with Pam. When he was diagnosed with lymphoma, Pam was heartbroken and knew that she was having to face a very difficult decision.

I walked home from work thinking about Henry and his transition to the world beyond. I knew we would be facing similar decisions eventually with our 16 year old cats, Angel and Shadow. As I walked in the door, I was greeted with a Monarch that had emerged and was ready to become a part of Henry's celebration of life.

Pam's husband, Stephen had lovingly created a small wooden box and lined it with a doggie blanket with paw prints on it. Henry was placed in the box along with doggie treats and Rose petals. There were tears of both sadness and joy as memories floated around the room. The Monarch eagerly flew towards the sunlight streaming in through the window as music played and poems were read. It was a wonderful send off for Henry.

August 5, 2018

Today, Henry was laid to rest in the garden that he loved. It was a beautiful summer day.

I received this text from Pam.

One of Henry's butterflies was out this morning!! They went into chrysalis the night before I found out he had lymphoma and emerged the morning after he took flight!! Another monarch magic story Barb 🦋 🖤 🐾

Photo Credit: Pamela Gerrand

September 17, 2018

Pam posted this Monarch encounter on Facebook. Wow!

Barbara J. Hacking

"So grateful for this magical Monarch moment yesterday. She hovered, circled and stayed for a good long while. Monarch Messengers bring smiles from beyond the veil."

Photo Credit: Ayrlie MacEachern

18

Five Years Ago

August 5, 2018

This came up on my Facebook memories today. It was a huge reminder that we have come a long way in a relatively short period of time!

Only four Monarchs! It was very scary! I think we only saw 14 that year in total. Mark and I were searching for them in places we had seen them in the past and they just weren't to be found. The following winter, revealed the lowest Monarch population in the Mexican overwintering grounds ever!

Barb Hacking
August 5, 2013 ·

Here is the 4th Monarch butterfly I have seen this year. It was nectaring in the Shakespearean Gardens peacefully.

This is only five years ago! I was ecstatic to see my 4th Monarch. I can remember being so excited as Monarchs were a rare sight!

This is before milkweed was taken off the noxious weed list (at least here in the province of Ontario, Canada) and before people were aware that

Barbara J. Hacking

Monarchs needed some help along with the bees. This summer is like a breath of fresh air seeing many more Monarchs.

Last summer, here in Ontario, Canada, more Monarchs were observed, but the count in Mexico taken last Winter claimed that the population was down fifteen percent since the previous year. This is definitely not the news we wanted to hear.

Canada, the United States and Mexico must all work cooperatively together. This tri-county migration of the Monarch is dependent on all of us.

Remember to plant milkweed and other native nectar plants for all pollinators, especially if you live in a place along their migratory path. The Monarchs that I happened to see in the Summer of 2015 were all in pollinator gardens, so it shows that if you plant for them, they will come!

19

Ev's 65th Birthday

August 5, 2018

Yesterday I took two Monarchs to my friend Ev to celebrate her birthday along with Pauline, her sister. When I discovered it was her 65th, I felt it should be an even bigger celebration.

When I returned home, I discovered eleven Monarchs had eclosed while I was out.

Mmmm! $6 + 5 = 11$.

I quickly arranged to meet with Ev the next morning at 11:00 to have a special release with several of her grandchildren and friends.

Again, it was a perfect morning to release butterflies and Ev's place in the country at Avonbank was an exquisite location. Any Monarch released here would be in their glory with fresh country air and sunshine. The release took place surrounded by the beautiful grove of trees, planted by Ev in memory of her family's loved ones.

That afternoon, we were sitting on her porch and discovered that her field right in front of us, was loaded with tender, young milkweed plants. They were hidden treasures among the other taller plants. Much of the milkweed was passed its prime now so this was a real find.

Ev was about to embark on her first Monarch egg hunting expedition. We were happy to find that a Mama Monarch had located her plants and left many gifts. We even found a few caterpillars. One was bigger than the tiny plant it was on.

Ev was excited and looking forward to sharing her new knowledge with her grandchildren. I'm sure they will look back one day with many cherished memories of their Monarch days with their Nana. Time spent with children discovering nature is never wasted!

When I returned home from Ev's, there were five more Monarchs waiting for me to release them. I drove over to Ted's garden and met a lovely family with two children from Nicaragua. They spoke Spanish and I told them the Monarchs understood their language as they migrated to Mexico each Winter. We had a good chuckle and they were delighted to help me! I forgot my camera but I will remember the smiles those kids had which of course made their parents smile.

20

Poop

August 6, 2018

I received this message from Ev which made me laugh.

"My caterpillar pooped, and I was excited to see that this morning!"

I was happy to hear that, as she will get a lot more excitement in her life if she raises caterpillars.

Monarchs eat a LOT and therefore, poop a LOT! That's really all they do from the time their egg hatches until they search for a suitable place to make their chrysalis.

Their first meal is their egg shell. Then they begin to munch on the leaf their mother chose especially for them. She knows that each of her babies will require a lot of Milkweed to grow and survive, therefore she usually, but not always, lays only one egg on a plant. It is most often firmly adhered to the underside of the leaf where it is protected from rain. This is the first year I noticed Monarchs laying multiple eggs on the flower buds.

Barbara J. Hacking

I used to tell my students that, "What goes in, must come out!"

Here is the scoop about caterpillar poop!

The more they eat, the more they grow!
The more they grow, the more they eat!
The more they eat, the more they poop!
And
The more they grow, the bigger the poop gets!

As I write this, Mark is chiming in,

"The more they poop, the better they feel!
So let's have Milkweed at every meal"

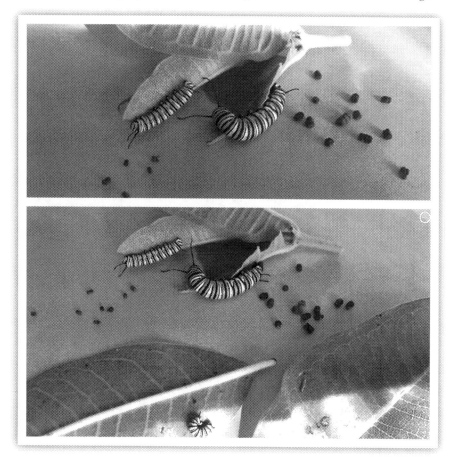

As one of Dr. Seuss' characters said,

"In my world, everyone's a pony and they all eat rainbows and poop butterflies."

21

Monarch Caterpillars are Fussy Eaters

August 5, 2018

Monarch caterpillars only dine on milkweed. When it was considered a noxious weed, that presented a major problem for them. **No Milkweed = No Monarchs**

When we remove any animal from Nature, it is critical that we treat it with respect, protect it, learn from it and then return it back unharmed. Each type of caterpillar eats a certain type of food. With the help of the Internet, it is easy to make sure we know what specific food it eats.

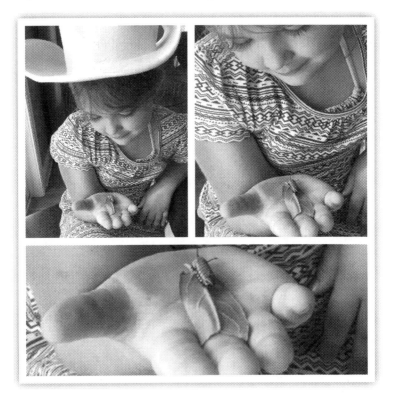

I once loaned one of my caterpillar enclosures to a person and gave them their very own caterpillar, along with detailed instructions. They assured me that they knew what milkweed was and where to get some to continue feeding the growing caterpillar.

A short time later, they returned the container back to me and had thought the caterpillar had escaped. When I opened it up there was a maple leaf lying on the bottom. On the dome-shaped lid was the tiniest chrysalis I had ever seen.

I think she fed maple leaves to the caterpillar. Of course the caterpillar did not have enough food to continue growing, so decided to pupate. (Enter the chrysalis stage)

I didn't know whether or not it would survive, but... it did! It was the tiniest Monarch I had ever seen and luckily, perfect in every way!

The moral of the story is to make sure you have the time and knowledge to keep the animal out of harm's way. If not, it's best to leave it where you found it.

22

Birthday Butterflies

August 6, 2018 (8:00 a.m.)

Today, my great niece turns 9 and she is on holidays enjoying the east coast. We were sad that we would be apart on her special day.

Weeks ago, she ran out of our house looking for Monarch eggs in our Milkweed patch. She found more than nine and quickly proclaimed that her birthday wish was to release nine butterflies. Last year, she was delighted to release eight. Then she sadly realized she would be on her holidays.

Last night, I gave a Monarch a wee kiss and sent it off on its way. Hopefully today, she will see a Monarch and be reminded that although we are not together, I am thinking of her! When she returns, I'm sure nine special Monarchs will be waiting for her.

August 6, 2018 (9:44 a.m.)

Serenity wasn't here but her nine Monarchs were! When I checked my Monarch house, I was completely dumbfounded! There were nine Monarchs all hanging from their chrysalid shells. I quickly snapped some photos and a video to send to Serenity.

Photo Credit: Kristi-Ann Sebben (center photo)

As I finished, one more eclosed for good luck and there looks like there will be four more before the day is out.

Timing butterflies to come out on a specific day is not easy. I guess if it's meant to be, it will happen.

23

I Thought I Saw a Butterfly

August 6, 2018

Tonight I was out for a walk with a friend. We thought we would explore some of the trails around Stratford that we had never walked. We strolled towards the Art Gallery and discovered a colourful garden. I thought I was imagining butterflies as I always seem to do, and guess what? I was right! Two beautiful butterflies were embedded in this exquisite garden. My, how I love this city and the amazing park staff!

My friend sent me a photo which really made me laugh. Amazing what a wet bathing suit can create.

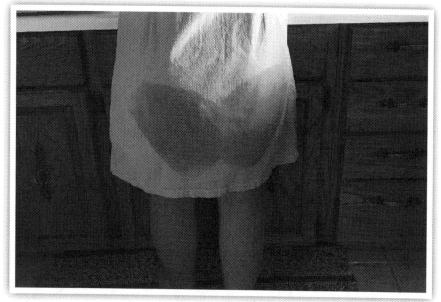

Photo Credit: Marg Hartman

This picture gives new meaning to the word "butt-erfly".

24

Happy Anniversary Rachel and Jeff

August 7, 2018

Rachel and Jeff's two birthday Monarchs arrived a day early to celebrate their third anniversary. A boy and a girl.

25

Field Trip - Bringing the World Together

August 7, 2018

"Diversity is about all of us, and about us having to figure out how to walk through this world together."

Jacqueline Woodson

Wow! Such a beautiful morning meeting International Students from China, Brazil and Russia! Their teachers Amy and Morgan took advantage of this gorgeous summer day to get their students out exploring the Ted Blowes Memorial Pollinator Peace Garden and extending their classroom lessons on the Monarch butterfly.

Each student was required to ask a question in English and I must admit I was extremely impressed with not only their English but the questions they asked.

Before the release, it was hard to get some of them to smile… but during and after the release that was no problem. The students sent messages back to their families with the help of the butterflies and also photos on their cell phones.

A Mother and her two children from England, who just happened to be visiting Ted's garden also happily joined in. Ted would have been so happy to see his garden being used to bring people from all over the world together learning about the environment.

Barbara J. Hacking

Like butterflies, people come in many colours, sizes and from many places.
That's what makes this world more beautiful!

26

Teach the Children Well;
They are the Future

August 7, 2018

I am reminded when I see a child's face light up when they see a jewel-like chrysalis or a butterfly fly for the first time, that we are responsible for teaching them to respect wildlife and take care of this Earth. We do that by our example and taking the time to show them this miraculous world.

Barbara J. Hacking

Yulia has been exposed to Monarchs from a very young age and enthusiastically displays no fear.

Photo Credit: Jennifer McCann (right)

The Internet is an amazing tool for finding information and presenting it; but it is not a substitute for being in nature and experiencing the real thing.

Watching a Monarch metamorphosize from an egg through its life cycle to an adult butterfly takes time and patience. Part of the excitement is the anticipation. The Internet brings about instant gratification, but is that always a good thing? Life isn't like that. On the other hand, Monarchs are not always available so we are lucky to have it to help educate.

I was excited to see this Facebook post tonight from a Mother of a child who was given some Monarch eggs by her Grandmother. The Grandmother is the sister of my friend Ev, who recently released some butterflies for her 65th Birthday. After the release, we had checked out milkweed plants and found some eggs.

"An extra big thank you to my Mom... for Ashlyn's new pet. We are not sure if it's a boy or a girl. I'm really not sure that he's as cute and lovable as Ashlyn seems to think he is. I'm really not sure what to do with him just yet, but he's now a member of our happy home. Ashlyn sits and talks to him and sings to him. I really hope it is a Monarch butterfly in the end or I'm going to have a very unhappy child. Our big vision is to watch him grow and develop into something other than a green blob on a leaf and be able to release him at the cemetery for my Dad. Fingers crossed!! Thanks Mom. You always seem to have the most creative ideas when it comes to fun. ☺"
Written by Jennifer Jablecki

Lucky Ashlyn is about to embark on an amazing adventure.

*

This special Grandmother, Ruth brought all 5 of her grandchildren to a butterfly release. She is creating special memories that they will never forget... and the best part, nature doesn't cost a cent.

I love the way Ruth has one hand helping Lincoln while holding baby Archer in the other.

*

Matthew was visiting his Grandmother from England. She had him at Stratford's amazing Art Gallery and he loved seeing the caterpillars that I couldn't leave in the car after an educational talk in Ted's garden. They accompanied me to this fine cultural experience. Matthew, was very intrigued. What wonderful Canadian memories his Grandmother Maureen has created!

August 13, 2018

Last night, I had the pleasure of meeting two year old Auraya. Her name is a combination of Aurora (Sleeping Beauty's name) and Freya (The Goddess of Nature). Her father James, is a single parent and I was most impressed by his excitement to introduce butterflies into her life. When I showed her a picture of a Monarch, she looked like the Goddess of Nature smiling on this beautiful creation.

We met at Ted's garden today and what a pleasure it was to introduce her to the world of butterflies. There were lots of pollinators flying around the sunny garden and we had 3 more to add.

At first, Auraya was a bit hesitant but with her Dad's gentle encouragement she was throwing kisses to the butterflies and could hardly wait to release them. It was a delight to see the transformation that happened quickly before our eyes. She eagerly checked out the butterfly carrier for more. Auraya's middle name is Sunshine and she definitely is a "Ray of Sunshine".

Kudos to James for taking the time to expose Auraya to the beauty of nature. Parents are great role models for their children.

While this release was happening, my friend Wendy's nephew came along with his son. It seems like only yesterday that Brent was a blonde-headed cutie. His son was the spitting image of days gone by. It was wonderful seeing these fathers guide their children into the world of nature so tenderly and gently.

Auraya was excited to share this experience with her new friend.

27

Feathers Falling from the Sky

August 7, 2018

I was shopping at Shannon's store and it was almost closing. I had a couple of butterflies to release and invited Olivia who works there to share the experience. I told her that perhaps she had someone close to her who had passed on, that she would like to honour.

A little while later we met at Ted's garden. It was an enchanting evening in many ways.

Olivia took the first butterfly over to the base of the waterfalls. She chose that spot because the Tiger Lillies reminded her of her Papa. She fondly remembers visiting him in the country and being in her glory as a child when there.

The Monarch was hesitant to leave her. I placed it on Olivia's heart and it moved upwards as she looked down upon it with loving eyes. Then the Monarch quickly kissed her chin and was off!

Within minutes of the release, an upside down butterfly cloud appeared in the sky. In the photos you can see Olivia's upside down butterfly tattoo on her arm.

Shortly thereafter, a fluffy feather fell from the sky and landed between us. It was amazing! Olivia picked it up as a souvenir of her release.

When Olivia was ready to release the second one, beautiful little Claire came by with her parents and Grandpa. Olivia kindly shared her experience with this lovely wee one. It was amazing to watch as the butterfly took flight. Claire's Mother said she talked about the butterfly until they finally got her to go to sleep.

Olivia and I sat in Ted's garden and were intrigued by the hummingbird that appeared to nectar among the red flowers. Olivia's Papa had hummingbird feeders so this was a happy reminder of him.

Then dragonflies began to dance around us as the sun started to sink in the sky. I told her the story of how Pam had seen a red dragonfly shortly after her dear pet Henry had left this world. That same evening I had seen an orange dragonfly sitting outside our kitchen window as we ate our supper. I chuckled and said perhaps we would see a rainbow of dragonflies, yellow being next.

The very next day, I happened to visit the store and Olivia was leaving for her supper break. She rushed back into the store excited to announce there was a yellow dragonfly hovering over her car. Unbelievable! I managed to videotape it but it moved very quickly. It was hard to keep up with it.

Barbara J. Hacking

August 12, 2018

The other day I was at Shannon's store, and that yellow dragonfly zipped back and forth in front of the store for close to an hour. It reminded me of the Road Runner. I became frustrated trying to get a good photograph of it. I think it was dodging my camera on purpose.

Now we are looking for green, blue and purple dragonflies to complete the rainbow sightings.

I invite you to Google the meaning of these dragonflies. Very interesting indeed!

28

A Monarch Goes to Art Class

August 8, 2018

We had invited Amanda, our good friends' daughter to visit Stratford and be our house guest. We had several butterflies and Amanda released them at Ted's Garden.

She wanted to release one at the top of the bridge so up we went. As I walked up the cement steps, I found a folded piece of paper that had been rained upon. The word "butter" caught my eye. I picked it up and the words "When a Butterfly Speaks" was written on one side and Gros Morne, Newfoundland on the other. I showed Amanda and told her that was the name of my book. That was very strange. Why was it there? Was I directed to find it and why? The book hadn't even been published yet. This was extremely mysterious.

One of the butterflies wasn't ready to fly, so we took it with us to paint some ceramic bowls for a fundraiser. It ended up being a great conversation piece and inspired us to put butterflies on our creations.

29

Butterfly Season At Its Best

August 9, 2018

For the past week, I have had trouble keeping up writing about all the special moments the Monarchs have created. Wow! I feel like I am in Butterfly heaven. The people I have met and the magical Monarch moments we have shared have been incredible. I am hoping that I will be able to do the stories justice in future chapters. Where do I begin?

30

The Head Pops Off!

August 9, 2018

I've been doing this Monarch raising thing for a very long time and I've seen the caterpillars shed their skin many times.

Lately, I was wondering what happened to the skin, so when I caught a caterpillar in the act, I videotaped it. It looked like it was taking off a pair of black pants and dropping them on the floor. As soon as he was naked, his head popped off! It rolled off of the leaf it was on and onto my lap. It didn't do much else except sit on the leaf.

Then it did a 180 degree turn and sat there staring at the skin it had just shed. I turned away for just a moment and the skin disappeared, except for a tiny bit left on his plate. I assume he ate it, but I'll have to watch more closely the next time I come across a shedding caterpillar.

31

The Butterfly's Promise Revisited

August 9, 2018

Many years ago (1999), the words for the poem "The Butterfly's Promise" circulated furiously within my head until the only way to tame them was to write them down. Our 17 year old nephew had just passed away.

The Butterfly's Promise

When you left your earthly home the butterflies began to dance
And sang a little song of hope that there's a second chance
To live some place much better where there's no hurt or pain
The earth's great loss we feel today turns into heaven's gain.
The memories we'll always treasure and you'll live within our hearts.
Forever we will love you... Saying good-bye's the hardest part.
We'll miss your loving smile, your jokes, your laugh, your love
We know you'll look down from heaven and guide us from above.
Until we meet again when we leave our earthly home.
The journey will not be feared knowing we won't be alone.
Each time we see a butterfly floating through the air,
We'll hear it's whispered promise that you're waiting for us up there.
For death is nothing more than the time to spread our wings.
We'll soar above this earth towards bigger and better things.

Written by Barb Hacking

Through the years, this poem has been a gift to many grieving people and has been received favourably. It was read at both of my parent's funerals. My daughter, who is a nurse, made notecards with it to give to families who have lost a loved one. I self published it to give it to people in times of grief. I believe it was my first experience at channeling.

Lately, I have been experiencing butterfly releases with people who are deeply grieving the loss of a loved one. I have come to realize how important it is to be open to the signs our loved ones send us. These signs can give great comfort at a time of deep sorrow.

I have seen feathers fall from the sky and land at people's feet immediately after releasing a butterfly. I have seen clouds transform into hearts, butterflies and angels and then disappear as quickly as they came. I have seen dragonflies circle a person until they can't help but notice. Rainbows have appeared without rain. A gentle breeze will all of a sudden place a kiss upon a cheek. Each release is unique and special.

Yesterday, I was leaving my brother Bruce's house and was telling my sister-in-law, Linda about how one medium had said that our Mother was surrounded by white butterflies and another medium more recently said she was sending butterflies to me. We were standing outside the house as I said good-bye and white butterflies kept flying around us. Perfectly timed divinely guided signs I would say.

There has been a white butterfly hanging around the flower basket on our front door as well.

Barbara J. Hacking

I have also come to realize that our loved ones want us to go on living our lives happily and sometimes we need to be reminded of that. That is the best present we can give them.

Today, three more verses came to be added to the original poem. They just flowed like a river. The words came quickly and I knew exactly where to place them.

The Butterfly's Promise (Two)

When you left your Earthly home, the butterflies began to dance
And sing a little song of hope that there's a second chance
To live somewhere much better where there's no hurt or pain.
The Earth's great loss we feel today turns into Heaven's gain.
The memories we'll always treasure and you'll live within our hearts.
Forever we will love you... Saying goodbye's the hardest part.
We'll miss your loving smile, your jokes, your laugh, your love.
We know you'll look down upon us and guide us from above.
Although we can not see you, we are open to each sign,
That you divinely send, to show you are just fine.
And when a gentle breeze lays a kiss upon our cheek,
We'll see that there are many ways we still can hear you speak.
Are you beyond that rainbow in a place we cannot see;
Looking down upon us, just watching quietly?
We cherish our dear memories. They brighten up our day.
For true love never dies, just because you've gone away.
The best gift we can give you now, is to live life with a song.
So we will do our best, not to be sad for long.
We hope our grief will lessen and we'll cry happy tears
When we hear your name; It'll be music to our ears.
We will come to realize that grief is the price for love
The two are so connected; like a hand inside a glove.
As colours melt together to begin a brand new day. Your love shines upon
us and we know you are okay.
Until we meet again, when we leave our Earthly home.
The journey won't be feared, knowing we won't be alone.
As the Sun routinely sets and another day goes by.
It takes us one step closer to our reunion in the sky.
Each time we see a butterfly, floating through the air,
We'll hear its whispered promise, that you're waiting for us up there.
A butterfly is a little piece of Heaven here on Earth.
It reminds us there's a special place where we're given our rebirth.
For death is nothing more than the time to spread our wings.
We'll soar above this Earth, towards bigger and better things.

Barbara J. Hacking

August 11, 2018

Another verse was added today. The original poem was written almost twenty years ago, so I guess it was time for an update.

October 9, 2018

You may have noticed that this was written after I thought I had finished the book. After an exciting day, this past Friday when I wrote the ending to this book, I truly felt done. This was so unlike my first book which didn't want to end. It was Thanksgiving weekend and I was truly grateful. I was enjoying the freedom of not having thoughts bubbling in my head. Saturday, Sunday and Monday went by and I didn't write. It felt foreign after 20+ months of continuous guided writing.

Well today, I awoke and I was thinking about my friend Lisa whose husband, Allan passed away in a plane accident in June, 2017. I thought about all the signs that have miraculously appeared since his passing. Lisa and I sometimes see the same signs even though we are in different places. It is these occurrences that have helped create the new verse in "The Butterfly's Promise" about divinely sent signs and being open to them.

One day I posted on Facebook a photo of some beautiful clouds that I just loved. Lisa quickly messaged me and told me she had seen the same clouds at her house. Little did I know there was an upside down Capital A (A for Allan). Lisa had seen it right away. When we took a closer look, we saw an angel-looking figure within the A. I received a message from another friend that she could see a man's face and she was right. Lisa and I both witnessed a plane drive into the A when we were observing the clouds although we were at our own homes.

When editing I took a closer look at the photos and saw a heart to the right of the upside down A and the cloud to the left reminds me of a plane soaring upwards.(Bottom photo)

Well that was the beginning of a whole series of signs. It makes total sense that a pilot who loved flying would send messages in the sky.

Shortly thereafter, I saw a strange cloud configuration as I walked home from work one day. To me it looked like "I♥L". I quickly sent it to Lisa.

One day Lisa sent me a video she had taken a while back. She had written Allan's name in the sand at a beach and noticed orbs floating around the writing. Lisa had been told by a medium that Allan was sending her lots of signs and to look for these orbs. When I took a closer look at the sky in the video I could see an angel cloud too. The more I looked at the video, the more I saw in the clouds.

When Lisa released the first butterfly of the season this past summer, just minutes before, Mark and I saw a cloud shaped like a plane.

When Mark and I were in France at Versailles, we saw a very clear A in the sky being created by planes as we watched the sun set. This seems to be Allan's favourite way of getting our attention.

This past weekend, Allan's young granddaughter discovered not one dime but two in unexpected places. She placed them on a shelf she had reserved for her memories of her Papa. It was Thanksgiving and these signs were a blessing as the family faced yet another holiday without Allan.

Lisa sees dimes in many unexpected places, such as shoes. In fact, she had collected enough to fill a mug half full.

Mark and I were at Point Pelee National Park, shortly after Allan passed away and the first thing I saw was a huge piece of driftwood in the shape of an A. Mark was photographing the sky and discovered an A. There was an airplane in the photo too. Unbelievable!

Another evening very recently, I saw another upside down A and Lisa had seen it too. It was the evening of the day Mark fell from the roof. A reminder that life is precious.

I saw a friend's post from California and saw the upside down A in the corner.

Lisa is so open to all these signs from Allan. She continues to be a woman of strength, faith and positivity. Lisa's friends are constantly amazed by her courage and ability to grow through her challenges. She helps others realize that life is precious and encourages us to make each moment count.

Lisa started a Facebook page, "Figuring Out Widowhood, One Step At A Time". As the title says, there are no set rules for grieving. Each day can be very different. Each person's process can be different. Lisa freely shares her thoughts, feelings and experiences and helps others grieving the loss of a loved one.

When I see this smiling photo of Lisa with that sparkle in her eyes, I know that Allan lives on in her heart. He will be smiling too.

My dear friend, Joy Depatie, who has just retired from working with many grieving people says,"If you accept the signs; you will receive even more." She reminds people to show gratitude for these gifts.

October 27, 2018

Lisa conveyed a happening from this summer that was amazing. She was out on Lake Huron in a boat quite a distance from the shore. Three Monarch butterflies appeared out of nowhere and flew around her. There were two other boats but the butterflies lingered in her direction for about an hour. Lisa had lost both of her parents and Allan in an 8 month period. She cherishes these special moments.

November 14, 2018

Today would have been my Dad's 104th Birthday. Another verse for "The Butterfly's Promise" has been percolating in my head for some time and today the words blended together in perfect harmony.

"And when a gentle breeze lays a kiss upon our cheek.

We'll see that there are many ways we still can hear you speak."

It reminds me of a time shortly after my Dad passed away. We were celebrating my Uncle John's birthday. All of a sudden, a nearby door blew open and the candles on the table went out as the breeze traveled like a bowling ball down a laneway. I couldn't help but feel my Dad wasn't going to miss the party.

If nothing else, it's times like these our loved ones come alive in our memories and it's our memories that keep them alive in our hearts.

November 29, 2018 (11/29/2018)

Here we are in the eleventh month. The 2 and 9 in the date add up to 11 as well as the numbers in the year. I woke up this morning and made the final adjustments to the poem.

December 10, 2018

Today I heard "The Butterfly's Promise" set to music for the first time. Steve Adair has metamorphosed it into an exquisite song. Adding a butterfly video to it will be my next creative endeavour.

To listen to the original poem set to music check it out on YouTube. Https:// youtu.be/5NJdurxQI3E

Barbara J. Hacking

December 20, 2018

Lisa is handed another sign from a student on the playground. An early Christmas present, perhaps!

Photo Credit: Lisa Metevier

Author's Note:

I truly thought I had finished editing this book. I must admit I was worried that the channeled experiences and writing would stop now that this book was complete. Today proved me wrong.

January 25, 2019
My Mom's 103rd birthday. More signs!

After driving into Stratford last night at 11:11 p.m., Mark and I arrived home exhausted from 20+ hours of traveling. We had been on a Canary Island Cruise, full of amazing adventures. I awoke around 4:00 a.m. Mark who is always up in the wee hours of the morning beckoned me to come and see something unusual. I sit here at 4:44 a.m. writing about this very strange occurrence. Our living room is always shut off from the rest of the house so our two cats don't leave their fur all over. It has kind of become a family museum full of treasures from my parents' home and therefore, my childhood. Painted china her Mom and aunts had created in the late 1800's, are constant reminders of our family's past. What made this morning unusual was that the electric fireplace was on. We had this happen many times before. A medium had told us it was a friend's wife, who had passed on many years ago, making her presence known. We hadn't even told her about the fireplace lighting on its own, but she knew. This time it felt different. We had gone to bed just before midnight and the fireplace had not been on then. We would have noticed through the glass doors when we took the suitcases upstairs. When I entered the room, the first thing I noticed was my Mom's porcelain doll had fallen over on the couch. Then I remembered that today was January 25th. It would have been my dear Mother's 103rd birthday. I always feel close to my parents when in this room, and today I could feel their presence even more so. I sat down by the fire to write this story as our cats, Shadow and Angel meandered around the forbidden room. Shadow began to explore, particularly interested in circling around the top of a small table, housing a photo of my Mom with her doll in a wicker buggy and a snapshot taken when my parents became engaged. It was as if she could see something that we could not. She then settled on the arm of the couch right beside the photos.

I thought back to my Dad's 103rd birthday when I was visited by a white moth tapping at the kitchen window. It was the middle of November and very odd for this time of the year in Canada. This moth

Barbara J. Hacking

was persistent at getting our attention. A visitor such as this would be practically impossible in January, so a cozy fire was the perfect way to get our attention. Happy Birthday Mom! You have been gone for 9 years now, and I know your wisdom still guides me.

Time creates memories when are loved ones are here on Earth. Memories give us comfort when they are not.

January 26, 2019

Still recovering from the time change I went to bed last night at 7:00 p.m. I just couldn't keep my eyes open any longer after waking up so early yesterday. I awoke at 2:22 and then 3:33 and finally got up at 4:32. I felt there was something I was searching for but had no idea what it was. The triple numbers were appearing and the sequence of descending numbers in the time 4:32 seemed to be calling me to go back in time.

For some strange reason, I began to explore Facebook and noticed that a friend had liked my cover photo album. I didn't even know I had an album of this nature. As I scrolled through the photos, I came across this one.

Mark took it one day at sunset and I posted it as I loved it so much. I hadn't seen the Capital A, the heart on the right or the butterfly clouds on the left, but, I had been guided to find it today. Wow! We need to be open to these signs sent from those on the other side.

When I questioned Mark about this photo, he distinctly remembers taking it just up the road from Lisa's and Allan's home. I posted it on the 5th of June and the photo was dated. He checked when he took it and it was June 3, 2017; the day after Allan soared beyond the clouds.

What allowed me to find this photo on this day? Coincidence or divine guidance?

January 29, 2019

Today I was telling my friend, Teresa about Lisa's A clouds. She immediately made the connection between what I was telling her and the book she was reading by Jacqueline Davieau called "Inspiration From Above". I knew I needed to read it.

The very next day, Jacqueline's book was in my hands. I discovered that when her 22 year old son, Mario passed away, an A cloud appeared immediately after his service. (A for angel) There was an angel cloud above it. The photo she included was beautiful and seemed like déjà vu.

The A sign in the sky is very fitting for a young man whose dream while growing up was to build "Sky Cities" and was just months away from graduating with a degree in Construction Management.

I was in awe of Jacqueline's experiences and was beginning to have a better understanding of the messages we receive and the ways in which we receive them. The timing of receiving this book was impeccable and I'm sure divinely guided.

Full of gratitude for Jacqueline's gift that she has been courageous enough to share with the world, I felt the need to connect with her to thank her.

Barbara J. Hacking

When I contacted Jacqueline, she kindly responded quickly and we were able to have a wonderful conversation about divinely sent signs. I was grateful for this heartwarming connection.

> **"A miracle is when God bends the laws of nature on your behalf."**
>
> **Sister Kevin**

32

The Monarchs Crash a Birthday Party

August 10, 2018

I noticed before I walked to work, that four Monarchs had eclosed and would be ready by this evening to be set free. I had promised the Evan's family that I would contact them when I had four butterflies. A year ago, four beautiful butterflies soared above their home in memory of their dear Sydney.

Sydney passed away unexpectedly at the age of 2. The Evan's family has so graciously kept her memory alive with special events that benefit our world. Last year was The Random Acts of Kindness Day to celebrate her 10th birthday.

I contacted, Michelle to let her know I had some butterflies, but didn't hear back from her while I was at work.

As I walked home that evening, I saw blue balloons flying on a bench overlooking Lake Victoria which caught my attention. I then saw some children running towards me asking me if I had any butterflies. They had released some earlier this summer and I was happy to say that I did. I asked their mother and aunt, if they would be around in about 20 minutes. If so, I would walk home and drive back with the Monarchs.

When I arrived, there was a crowd of people down by the river, and I realized they were celebrating Foster William's and William Bear's 3rd Birthdays. That's why the balloons were there.

A mixture of emotions were felt on this gorgeous summer evening. "Bear" had passed away on the day of the twins' birth leaving behind a great sadness. Foster, is a curious, curly-topped youngster that has brought great joy to those who know him. It was bitter-sweet.

The kids were excited to send the butterflies up towards the heavens, thinking about Bear as they did so. Many butterfly clouds reflected down into the waters of Lake Victoria.

I am always amazed how the butterflies find their way into the right hands at the right moment.

"Butterflies are like angel kisses sent from heaven."

Malia Kirk

When you release a butterfly you are sending kisses right back.

33

Signs from Sydney

August 12, 2018

The day after the release for Foster and Bear, I heard from Michelle Evans. They had been on holidays, but she contacted me as soon as they had returned. They had been seeing many butterflies and two of them almost landed on them the day before. One even stayed for about 15 minutes. It sparked a conversation about how our loved ones send us signs from time to time.

Me: "I have admired your willingness to share your grief. It is so healing for others to see. I actually added 3 more verses to the Butterfly's Promise yesterday. I have been releasing many butterflies recently for people grieving huge losses and have come to the conclusion that these signs are sent from our loved ones to let us know they are in a great place and also they want us to live our lives joyfully, but keep them alive in our hearts. So the 3 verses are about being open to the signs they send and to be happy. I am so glad to hear that the butterflies found you yesterday even though we didn't get together. I have one out today and hopefully more. If not they hopefully will be out for tomorrow. I'll keep you posted! One for sure 🦋"

Michelle: "I know! It always amazes me. Every time I see a butterfly close by, I go, "Oh! There's a butterfly!" I just can't help it! I feel like it's a sign every time!"

Me: "Yes, recently after doing releases, I have witnessed clouds like hearts, butterflies and angels. I have seen feathers fall from the sky and land at our feet. I have seen dragonflies circling us. I don't believe they are coincidental."

Barbara J. Hacking

Michelle: "Yes to all those things! I often find feathers & dragonflies randomly appearing as well! It's so special ❤"

We set up a time to release Sydney's butterflies. By the time the next morning had rolled around, I had eight. Two for each member of the family.

Again, it was an exceptional morning at Ted's garden. There was a gorgeous Swallowtail visiting the flowers, as well as many other pollinators. A perfect day for Sydney's tribute.

October 19, 2018 (10/19/2018)

Today would have been Sydney's 11th Birthday. Just like last year, the Evans family created "Random Acts of Kindness Day" in memory of their dear daughter and sister. Many acts of kindness made this day special for so many people. It was amazing to participate.

Last year, I saw a Monarch butterfly in the Shakespearean gardens. It should have been off to Mexico but decided to stick around to celebrate Sydney's birthday.

This year, the Monarchs are long gone. In the garden I saw the flowers mimicking butterflies, a sign that said Sydney and exquisite clouds that reminded me of angels.

It was great to see the Evan's family smiling on this day.

Author's Note: It was Sydney's 11th birthday. The numbers of the month and date add up to 11 (1+0+1+9), as well as the numbers in the year. (2+0+1+8) Angel numbers!

February, 2019

This heartfelt piece of writing was written by Sydney's older brother, Eric, while in grade 8. I am proud to say that I had the pleasure of teaching Eric in my last grade 1 class.

Losing A Part of Myself

I remember as if it were yesterday, I was a young, proud and energetic kid at the age of 4 swinging with my little sister Sydney. The utmost important part of my life would be my childhood, living in a small house with a smaller backyard and a tiny fort with two swings. Everything felt right in the world. It was a bright day, not what you'd expect for a sad story. Little me, sitting in my toy room playing with my sister and our dog. It was so peaceful. We were giggling and our parents were in the kitchen making my favourite dinner - spaghetti! Without any warning my sister began throwing up, which at the age of 2 is nothing to be alarmed about. She remained ill all night and we chalked it up to the stomach flu. The next day, a Thursday, my Mom stayed home from work with us. We slept in and then got up like every other day. We played my Lightning McQueen video game, me in the front of the blow-up car and Sydney in the back. We had a great morning together, it was just another normal day in my life. That afternoon Sydney had a nap. When she woke up her heart was racing so fast and hard you could literally see it beating out of her chest. I've never been so scared in all my life. My parents dropped me off at my Uncle's and took my sister to the hospital. This would be the last time I would ever see my little sister awake. The next day my Papa picked me up and took me home. My sister and parents weren't there. When I asked where Sydney was my Papa and my Uncle Shawn looked at each other and said nothing. I was really missing my family but no one would tell me what was going on though I knew something was happening because everyone was worried and looked sad. The following day, on Saturday, my Papa and Uncle Shawn took me for a long car drive to see my family. It seemed to take forever to get there. When we finally arrived we were at a big hospital. It was huge! A lot of my family were there and my parents were so happy to see me. They looked tired and sad and they told me I would see Sydney when she was done with some tests. To pass the time I rode the elevators up and down with my Uncle Dan. At one point I got quite upset because I lost my toy marble down the elevator. Mom and Dad told me that Sydney was really sick, that her heart was failing and that she would need a heart transplant. I didn't really know what that meant and frankly, I didn't really care but everyone around me seemed sad. I just wanted to play with my sister again! Finally my Mom and Dad brought me to see my sister. Nothing could prepare me for the horrible sight. She was lying asleep in bed, she was all puffy and she had HUGE tubes stuck into her neck. Mom told me that the tubes were pumping her heart for her. I hugged her and held her hand for a while and then I went back into the hallway to ride the elevators again. We all went to get some lunch. There were a lot of people there to visit us! As we were finishing lunch the doctors came to get my parents. A long while later someone took me up to see my Mom and Dad. They were all alone in a room and crying. I sat on my Mom's lap and she said to me, "Sydney's really sick and she is going to go to heaven," I started crying right away and I said, "But I don't want her to go, I want to play with her some more!" My family all came to the hospital to say goodbye. It was the saddest moment of my life. That happened nine years ago and we still miss her with great sorrow. This tragedy changed my family. We have tried to find positives amongst the sadness. We're open about Sydney and what happened, we're more caring towards others and we help others as much as we can. We've felt pain no others should have to feel. My sister Aubrey who was born two years later in 2011 never got to meet Sydney but she feels like she knew her and talks about her all of the time. She will always be a part of our family. Sydney's passing has taught me to cherish the time we have with loved ones because you never know what tomorrow will bring. We've made a decision as a family to turn our tragedy and sadness into something positive by doing Random Acts of Kindness on Sydney's birthday. We celebrate Sydney and her life and hopefully make a difference in someone else's life.

> **"Too often we underestimate the power of a touch, a smile, a kind word, a listening ear, an honest compliment, or the smallest act of caring, all of which have the power to turn a life around."**
>
> **Leo Buscaglia**

34

"Monarch Watch" Tags Are Here!

August 13, 2018

Yesterday, I received a yellow envelope from Monarch Watch, filled with migration tags, which signaled that the Monarchs will soon be on their way south to their overwintering grounds in Mexico.

A tag is placed on the lower wing carrying a tracking number registered with the organization in the United States; Monarch Watch. Information such as sex, whether it was reared or wild, where and when it was tagged and by whom is all collected. When a tagged butterfly is found, scientists will be able to use this information to learn more about migration patterns and behaviour.

I am always fascinated at the fact that none of these Monarchs have been to Mexico before but find their way there to roost in the Oyamel Fir tree forests of the mountains located in Central Mexico. It is the grandchildren and great grandchildren of these Monarchs, that will return to us here in Canada next Spring.

During the past week, there have been reports that the Monarchs have started their migration. I must admit, it made me a bit sad as that means the beloved Monarchs are beginning to leave us. Last year, my final Monarch was seen on October 22nd here in Stratford, Ontario, which is very late.

This was the last Monarch I had the pleasure of seeing during the Fall of 2017. It was enjoying the Lantana flowers in the beautiful Shakespearean Gardens, in Stratford, Ontario.

We are seeing a mixture right now of the summer generation and those that will migrate called the Super Generation. Just the other day, I witnessed a Mama Monarch whose wings were missing many of its scales, flying from milkweed to milkweed happily depositing eggs. That means we will be seeing Monarchs for at least another month, all being well.

Barbara J. Hacking

This female Monarch lays her eggs on the underside of a milkweed leaf by tucking her abdomen under it.

When I was teaching, I had tagged some Monarchs to show my students how research was conducted. When I retired from teaching in June, 2012, there were so few. You can't tag them, if they aren't here! Mark only found one caterpillar that Fall and that was after looking extensively in many places.

Last summer, (2017), people in Ontario were seeing more Monarch butterflies again and happily this summer there are even more. I am looking forward to tagging them once again! Who knows? Perhaps when I visit Mexico in February, I will see one of these butterflies.

Tagging has been an incredible tool to help scientists learn more about this amazing insect that migrates many thousands of kilometres to Mexico. It is the Citizen Scientists such as Donald Davis, Terry Whitham, Bruce Parker and others along the migration route that spend many hours in the Fall, tagging.

35

Beyond Coincidence

August 14, 2018. (6:11 a.m.)

"There is a voice that doesn't use words. Listen!"

Rumi (1207-1273)

The next story is very complex as it involves many people and many exciting events that happened in a very short period of time. I wasn't quite sure how to get it all down on paper and do it justice. I just had to trust that the story would materialize when the time was right. Bits and pieces of it have already surfaced in other chapters, but now the words are flowing. It's like a jigsaw puzzle and the pieces are starting to go together smoothly. I am hoping that I don't get to the end and find there are missing pieces. Lol!

The title has been percolating in my head as I have tried to sleep. I knew I needed to awaken and write it down, hoping the story would unravel and before I lost it forever.

Many months ago, back in January, my good friend, Ev's sister, Pauline, lost her dear husband, Rick (he was also known as Jack). He was only 68 years old. Pauline lost her husband, Jennifer, her daughter lost her Father and Ashlyn, her granddaughter lost her Grandpa. Their hearts were broken from this huge loss.

A couple of weeks ago, Ev invited me to her sister's place to see her beautiful property in the country. I asked Ev if Pauline would like to release a Monarch in memory of Rick, as it sounded like her grounds would be heaven for a fluttering butterfly.

At first, Ev didn't hesitate to say yes, but then she remembered how the butterfly symbol had become a sad reminder for their family, especially for Jennifer, during the five months Rick was in the hospital. Any time a person passed away, a picture of a butterfly was put on the person's door. Every time Rick's door was closed he would ask if there was a butterfly on it.

Jennifer best describes this difficult time.

"I once loved the beauty of the butterfly. After spending 5 months with my dad at the hospital, my love quickly grew into a dislike. Every time someone would pass away, they would post a picture of a butterfly on the door, as a symbol for staff. Every day we saw those pictures and it killed me inside. We knew my dad would be a butterfly far sooner than any of us were ready to admit. I dreaded the day he became one. I asked the staff to not post a pic on his door. The day we took him home for his final journey, he said to me as we were leaving the hospital, "At least I won't become a butterfly here but instead in my own home." Every time I have seen a picture of a butterfly since, it still tugs at my heart."

Since Ev's birthday had been the day before, I was guided to take two butterflies to help her celebrate, hoping that Pauline would find it a positive experience. I had to trust that the Monarchs would work their magic... and they did!

It was a lovely afternoon, and as we walked around Pauline's beautiful property we discovered lots of milkweed plants and even some gifts that a Monarch had left on them. Eggs! Both Ev and Pauline were thinking of their grandchildren and decided to gather a few for them. Little did they know the Monarch magic that would follow.

A few days later, Jennifer posted her thank you to her Mom for Ashlyn's eggs. One had hatched and created much excitement, not only for Ashlyn but her mother as well. (See story 26)

Jennifer and I then connected on Facebook. She messaged me the following.

"I have seen the beauty of the butterflies in my own yard and at my Mom's and over the past few months, I have let my resentment go. Having this little creature in my house has made me smile. I look forward to watching him grow and love Ashlyn's idea of letting him go in the cemetery when he's ready. Thank you again for what you do. My daughter is absolutely in love with him and a part of me is too."

The next morning, I had butterflies eclose and messaged Jennifer to see if her family would like to join me at the Ted Blowes Memorial Garden for a release in her Dad's honour. She didn't hesitate to say "Yes!"

These butterflies would soon be in the right hands.

Three generations gathered for the release of the butterflies at Ted's garden; Rick's wife, daughter and granddaughter. The weather cooperated and that evening was magical in many ways.

Ashlyn was excited to receive a caterpillar, ready to enter the chrysalis stage. She then chose to release her butterfly on the bridge. There were many butterfly clouds just waiting to be discovered in the sky and the bridge was the perfect spot to view them.

The smiles I saw on that perfect summer evening warmed my heart and I believe the butterfly symbol will have a new meaning for them all. These three, strong and beautiful women will help each other. The bond they share was beautiful to watch.

When I returned home from the garden, I received a lovely message from Pauline telling me that today was the 50th anniversary of her first date with Rick. Tears of joy fell down my cheeks as I realized that tonight was the perfect time for the butterfly release. These butterflies always seem to find their way into the right hands at the right moment. I have to wonder if Rick had arranged this especially for his lovely wife. These events manifested so quickly and amazingly that I wouldn't doubt it for a second.

As I finished this story, I received this message from Jennifer. "Ashlyn's caterpillar has transformed into its chrysalis."

Why is it that I am not surprised?

December 8, 2018

This Facebook post by Jennifer was amazing to see.

Putting up our Christmas tree today was an emotional challenge..and a physical one that my sister can remedy in the morning. This year we decided not to put an angel or a star on top but instead butterflies. One that is papa purple my dads favourite colour in memory of him and a white one in memory of all of our other family and friends who grew their wings over the many years. Last year at this time I probably would have hit someone at the mere mention of doing so. Tonight I'm grateful for the memories and experiences we have had that have brought me to a place of peace.

Photo Credit: Jennifer Jablecki

Jennifer is so open to the signs her dear Dad sends to let her know he is fine. Often he comes to her in her dreams. One night he even alerted her to smoking curtains as she slept.

Jennifer laughed as she told me about giving him $60 worth of dimes when he passed away. She has not been disappointed as her family continuously finds dimes in unexpected places.

January 26. 2019

Today is the first anniversary of Rick's passing. During the past year Pauline has been gifted with a beautiful, crimson cardinal that comes knocking on her window almost daily. He has even been known to come knocking on her door. What a wondrous occurrence!

Photo Credit: Pauline Jablecki

On Rick's birthday after he left this Earth, his family was missing him immensely. Ashlyn knew her Grandmother was having a difficult time, so asked for a special sign; one that they would know was for her. The very next day, Pauline was greeted with a cardinal knocking at her window trying to get in. It has stayed with her ever since, except for a couple of weeks last summer. It's like the gift that keeps on giving.

Another piece of the story showed up knocking on our door. Going back to August 11th, just a few days ago, Ev was having a Tacky Party. A Tacky Party you may ask? Well, everyone dressed in a tacky way and brought a tacky gift to share. A good time was had by all!

I had the pleasure of meeting Laurel, who had recently lost her sister and best friend. She had been given a copy of the poem, "The Butterfly's Promise", by Pauline and we were chatting about Pauline's remarkable release. Now, when it came to choosing from the pile of tacky gifts, Laurel happened to choose what I brought, which tied in nicely with our earlier conversation. It actually was amazing, since there were twenty-five other gifts she could have chosen from and all the gifts were wrapped!

It was a container with a Monarch butterfly to release. Someone shouted out when she opened it, "A butterfly isn't tacky!"

I smiled and said, "No! But asking for the container back, is!"

We all laughed and Laurel, although she lived out of town promised to return it after releasing the butterfly. It was too dark to release it right away.

So here she was returning the container just minutes after I had finished writing Pauline's family story. I was getting dressed for work, but went running out of the house to see Laurel before she drove away. I was excited to hear how her release went.

She had decided to let it free on her farm in memory of her dear sister. The next day she was talking on the phone and a Monarch went flying by her window. It was a happy reminder of the "Butterfly's Promise" and a bit of foreshadowing of things to come.

September 10, 2018

I received an email from Laurel today telling me about the Monarch that landed on her foot, not once but twice. She commented that it gave her such a peaceful and poignant feeling at the same time. This was a moment where opposite emotions collided. Happiness at seeing the sign but a reminder of the great loss of a loved one. She was able to take a photo and sees a Monarch often. Her young grandson just said, "Hi Aunt Dorothy!" when he saw it.

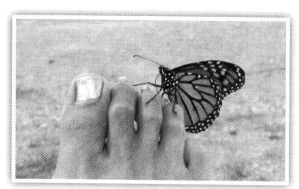

Photo Credit: Laurel Laughton

Barbara J. Hacking

September 11, 2018

Laurel emailed me once again telling me about yet another encounter with a Monarch. While she was sitting on the beach, a Monarch flew by and landed on the sand by her chair. She just laughed and said, "Oh Dorothy, that can't be you! It is too far to fly to come for a visit."

Laurel said the only other insects there that day were mosquitoes and sandflies.

Author's Note: I wrote Laurel back stating that she had definitely been touched by Monarch Magic. I just love it when that happens!!! It all started with a Monarch that mysteriously found its way into her life.

August 26, 2018

I was so happy to receive this message this morning from my friend, Dee, who has been touched by Monarch Magic for a while now. She was also the one who provided the journal I began writing "When a Butterfly Speaks... Whispered Life Lessons" in, after I happened to win it.

"Hey girl.... gotta share with you. Might even put this story in your butterfly blog online. I was on a pontoon boat this morning.... out on the lake with about a dozen others. Someone behind me told me that I had a butterfly over the top of my head. I looked up and there it was.... it fluttered away as the boat was moving at the time. About 5 minutes later... it returned and my heart leapt..... it flew by me again... not going near ANYONE else... and I watched it head across the lake. I thought to myself... if it appears again... that will make 3 and I must be getting a message. Honest.... it came back about 10 min later and HOVERED over my extended hand as if trying to land on me. I was speechless for the next half hour. OMG.... totally stunned.... Oh.... and it was a Monarch!"

My response to her was, "Monarch magic!!! Monarch miracles!!! I don't doubt it for a second."

Dee wondered, "Any thoughts on the message?? I was thinking how overall happy I was sitting on that boat..... the breeze and the water and how I love life. Do butterflies or Monarchs have specific messages..... like dragonflies, etc?"

Butterflies symbolize many things and bring forth many silent messages if we are open to them. I told Dee that perhaps it was reminding her of the huge transformation she was undergoing.

Dee replied, "I can still see the butterfly hovering over my fingertips... but the boat was moving. I wonder if it would have landed on my hand, if it had been still? The one amazing thing is that NOBODY else was visited.... it came to ME all three times."

"I am not surprised!" I told Dee, "They know who loves them. It will be permanently captured in your mind's camera. Love it!!! I am not surprised the butterflies are following you! Who wouldn't?"

36

Sunrise, Sunset

August 15, 2018 7:00 a.m.

"The breeze at dawn has secrets to tell you. Don't go back to sleep."

Rumi

Last evening I was looking at some of the photos we have on our computer. Mark being an early riser often goes off in search of beautiful sunrise scenes. I came across one that looks like there is a butterfly floating in the air. I just love it! It will definitely be in "The Butterfly's Promise" book I'm working on. It also inspired me to add one more verse to the poem. If you go back to Story 31, I bet you can figure out which verse was added this morning.

August 15, 2018 (Just before midnight).

Today was incredible! From morning until night, each butterfly found its way into the person's hands and heart that needed it.

I added more verses to "The Butterfly's Promise ". This morning the verse was about the Sun rising and tonight's verse was about the Sun setting. These are parts of nature that are cyclical and beautiful beyond words, just like a butterfly.

The sunset reminds us that the darkness won't be forever and the sunrise reminds us of that promise fulfilled. This is one of nature's gifts; free of charge, there for everyone and shared with the rest of the world.

I always love the fact that the sunrise is a reminder that each new day is a gift with no mistakes in it.

37

Butterflies on the Bucket List

August 15, 2018 11:00 a.m.

When I got into the car to go to Ted's Garden I couldn't believe all the angel numbers on my dashboard. What they meant I did not know but I knew some miracles/synchronicities were about to materialize.

How does one turn their kids' summer vacation into fun and excitement? Make a bucket list at the beginning and do your best to check off as many as you can.

It can be as simple as using chopsticks! As exotic as hugging a giraffe! What about releasing a Monarch butterfly?

Michelle and her daughters, Aveleen and Keara have been spending their summer doing just that. This morning they met at Ted's garden to make a special wish as they let their butterfly go.

When their butterflies were free they thought perhaps it would be something their Nana would like to do, since she was a butterfly lover. I am always impressed when young people think of others. I told them we could easily make that happen.

12:00 p.m.

When I arrived home, I found two more Monarchs out of their chrysalids waiting for their wings to dry. I trusted that before the end of the day, I would know who they belonged to.

2:00 p.m.

I was right! I received a message from Michelle saying it was 13 years ago to the day that their Nana said goodbye to her Mother for the last time, in Ireland. She also believes that butterflies are messengers sent by angels. So I'm pretty sure the angels manifested this release on this special day of remembering. It was amazing that I just happened to run into Michelle yesterday, when I hadn't seen her for months.

Of course it had to happen today to make it absolutely perfect. Nana was out getting groceries and I had a commitment that evening at 5:00 p.m., so we were hoping it would all work out. It did!

We met once again at Ted's garden. It was a pleasure to chat with Barbara, with her delightful Irish accent, as she chose to release the butterfly among the exquisite flowers. The butterfly took its time when the lid was lifted. I placed it on Barbara's heart and then it took off into the air. It circled around her and then it was gone, up to the top of a tree. The delicate white butterflies were present too. In fact, there was one that raced past us and took us by surprise. Michelle could even feel the breeze it created.

Just minutes after Michelle messaged me that Nana would be available to do a release, I was asked by a friend, if by chance, there was a butterfly for Angie who had just said a sad goodbye to her cat. I took it over right away and was pleased that the butterfly was ready to fly at the right moment... and it matched Angie's tattoo exactly.

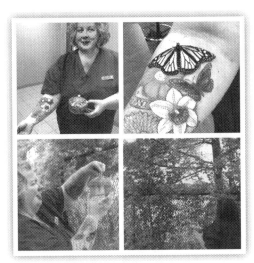

The butterflies had found their way into the right hands once again.

I am happy to say a new little kitten found its way into Angie's heart and home. Amazingly, it is orange like the Monarch.

August 16, 2018

The very next day, I received a copy of this message from Michelle. It was written by Barbara's sister in Ireland, in response to seeing the photos and video of her Monarch butterfly release, the day before. Wow! The power of the Internet!

"MEMORIES.... and how one beautiful image can lead to the revival of the memories of long ago. Yesterday, my family throughout the world commemorated the passing of our dear mother. Whilst she passed away on the 13th of August, we as a family, were mindful of Mam's devotion to Our Blessed Lady, and it was very comforting to us when we said our last good-byes to her, on the 15th of August - . The Feast of the Assumption of our Blessed Lady into Heaven - and so that date now holds added poignancy for us all. Last night, I was very moved by a video clip of my lovely sister Barbara Flood, as she lovingly released a home-reared Monarch butterfly into the wild, with heartfelt reverence and reflection, many miles away, in remembrance of Mam. The image remained with me throughout the night and brought to mind a poem my Dad had learned in Broadford National School, back in the early 1900's and later taught to me when I was a child.... It was the image of the butterfly that stirred the memory of the reference to the Pimpernel butterfly in the poem, and of course the memory of my dad patiently explaining to me what a Pimpernel actually was. Daddy would recite the poem as it had been taught to him and it was my first introduction to poetic licence, because in the opening line the word WIND was pronounced WINDE.... and I remember being intrigued by this aberration, yet accepted it without question. The poem was written by a very learned man... he invented the vaccine for smallpox, if I'm not mistaken (Jenner?) but he wrote this as a lighthearted "list of excuses" for NOT accepting an invitation to go out with some friends!! Should any of my "younger" relations and friends read this poem, you will learn that, prior to televised or "online" weather forecasts, these "signs" from nature were the means by which my Dad and others of his generation, would tell if it was going to be a suitable day to go to the bog to "save the turf", or should he begin the clipping and shaping of our ornamental hedges... he was a topiarist and he didn't know it - I don't think the word had even been invented (!).... Many is the time I heard him say, with great disdain, "de'clerta God, (translates as -- I declare to God!) the cattle are {lying}

119

down in Cosgrove's field..... isn't that dreadful' "...It was NOT gonna be a good day - in more ways than one!! Once Mam saw and heard this, her poor heart would sink.

The swallows are flying low - so no chance of hanging out her sheets on the line.. a disgruntled husband who will insist on bringing every bicycle in the place to overhaul on our small kitchen floor - no bog or garden today - and add to that a "herd" of unruly, bored and mischievous children....... Is it any wonder we all are confident in the knowledge that our dear Mother was assumed directly to heaven as we said goodbye to her on 15 August, 2005?

It is equally poignant that Daddy passed away on Easter Saturday - a festive time, a time of renewed faith, new life, new beginnings and great hope. I know the swallows are flying high, the Pimpernels (and Monarchs) are displaying their wondrous wings and the sun is shining brightly upon both of them today and always. God bless, my family and friends. It's time for me to step off memory lane for now because "there's great dryin' out" today and it'd be a shame to waste it! I'm keepin' an eye on the cattle "a-douth" (outside) in the field, just in case... Rest in peace Mam and Dad. Always remembered and dearly loved. 💔"

Written by Adrienne De Lacy from Moyville, Ireland. She is the youngest sister of 13 and still lives in the family home.

Mother mo chroi
(Gaelic, meaning "mother of my heart")...

Photo Credit: Joan Griffin

Such a beautiful tribute to her Mam and so exquisitely written!

Perhaps it is true what the Chaos Theory says,

"Something as small as a flutter of a butterfly's wing can ultimately cause a typhoon halfway around the world." In this case it produced a beautiful heartfelt piece of writing.

Later on, I returned home from work to find a beautifully decorated envelope adorned with roses, that had come in the mail from the Monastery of Mount Carmel. It was almost too perfect to open, but I did anyways. Inside, I discovered red rosary beads that matched the red roses on the envelope and they adorned a Saint Theresa medallion. The letter inside talked, coincidentally about Mothers and how they look out for their children. There was a pouch for the rosary beads with my name on it. I wasn't quite sure who sent them or why, but I knew they weren't for me. They were for Barbara, also known as Nana.

I hopped in the car and went directly to Michelle's. Nana lives two doors down and we quickly took the rosary beads to her. We all couldn't believe it.

Then Nana went inside and brought a framed certificate she had received that day, complete with roses and Saint Theresa's name and picture on it.

I just love Nana's reflection in this photo and I see a butterfly shape to the left of Saint Theresa's head.

Barbara J. Hacking

Michelle had sent me a photo earlier today of Nana's front lawn. There were dandelions growing in the shape of a butterfly. I couldn't see it then, but definitely could when I was there. Wow! That's all I can say!

Seeing all those angel numbers earlier truly were foreshadowing the miracles and synchronicities coming our way.

> **"May the wings of a butterfly touch the sun**
> **And find your shoulder to light on,**
> **To bring you luck, happiness and riches.**
> **Today, tomorrow and beyond."**
>
> **An Irish Blessing**

38

Triple Release

August 16, 2018

When my friend, Pam's beloved dog, Henry passed away, Pam was so filled with gratitude for the kindness shown by the staff at Coventry Animal Hospital. They came to her house and made these dark moments as comforting as possible. Pam was especially impressed, as many of the staff had recently lost pets of their own. I think it is safe to say, that people who work at a vet clinic have a special heart for animals, their health and their comfort.

Angela, one of the veterinarians, kindly arranged for three special butterflies to arrive at the clinic one evening for members of their staff who recently had to say goodbye to their fur babies.

We noticed one of the butterflies was larger than the others so decided to add a tag. It was probably one of the Super Generation. Who knows? Perhaps it will be found in Mexico.

It was raining and soon it would be dark, so the butterflies would spend some time with each person and their families before being released in the morning.

The releases allowed them to shed the tears they needed to shed and say goodbye in a comforting way. One of the butterflies even spent the night with a special little girl before flying off.

TAG:GKU.EDU
MONARCH WATCH
1-888-TAGGING
YAZ 416

39

Where There's a Will, There's a Way (Morgan's Monarch)

August 15, 2018

My daughter's sister-in-law messaged me this morning that her five year old daughter, Morgan had found an injured Monarch and she was determined to help it. Its wing was damaged and therefore it couldn't fly. They wanted to know how they could make its life better.

Rachel, my daughter happened to drop by their house and offered her assistance.

It was great to see someone so young want to help. Morgan did a great job feeding her butterfly and who knows what the future will hold for the butterfly… and for Morgan.

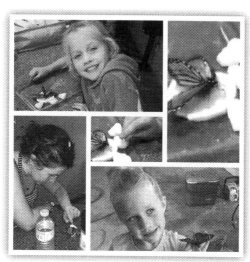

Photo Credit: Dina Swanson

Barbara J. Hacking

September 8, 2018

This one injured butterfly led Morgan and her family to enter the world of Monarch Magic. They recently moved to a farm and discovered they have fields laden with milkweed. This was such a great season to find the treasures they had right in their own backyard.

40

Imagination Revisited

August 16, 2018

I talked about imagination quite extensively in my first book, "When a Butterfly Speaks... Whispered Life Lessons". As an elementary school teacher for thirty years, I was immersed in the imaginative world of the child and the magical nature of being so. Perhaps, I have come to see things in a different way than most people, but I must admit it sure enhanced my life and makes it a lot of fun.

When it comes to butterflies, I see them everywhere! It reminds me of the saying,

> **"What you look for, you will find."**
>
> **(Sophocles, 496-406 B.C.)**

I see butterflies in flowers, rocks and even on a grape.

Barbara J. Hacking

October 28, 2018

Today I was preparing a salad for lunch with my best childhood friend, Caroline and her husband Gary, from Scotland. When I cut the tomato I saw a butterfly and laughed. Then I cut the stem off the cauliflower and saw another one. When I chopped the onion slices and lifted the chopper my imagination was working overtime. I guess I was really missing the Monarchs now that they were flying into Mexico.

December 8, 2018

I posted photos of the butterflies I found in the ice when I shoveled our driveway. They really are squirrel footprints. My friend Ev says I have magnetic eyes for butterflies. I think she is right!

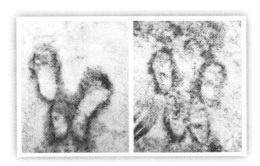

"Your imagination can lead you to a World of Worry or a World of Wonder. It's your choice."

Zen to Zany

41

The Importance of Forgiveness

"I can have peace of mind only when I forgive rather than judge."

Gerald Jampolsky

August 16, 2018

This summer I have witnessed many people release from their lives, that which no longer serves them, such as relationships, emotions or old habits.

When I had my wedding rings stolen I discovered the power of forgiveness. Every once in a while those feelings of resentment, anger and lack of trust resurface. I thought that perhaps a butterfly release for me would be helpful.

Barbara J. Hacking

October 11, 2018 (10/11/2018)

I received this beautiful story from Cathy Engelberger Kuczynski, from Pennsylvania.

For thirty years, Cathy watched her sister, Nancy battle a debilitating drug addiction. This was heartbreaking, as they were inseparable as children. They had grown apart through the years but her sister was determined to get back into her good graces. Cathy was reluctant to let her in, fearful of getting hurt once again by Nancy's actions.

One day in June, Nancy came to her with a Monarch caterpillar. She challenged Cathy to see if she could turn it into a butterfly.

Cathy lovingly kept it, fed it and before long she had herself a chrysalis. As the caterpillar developed into a butterfly, Cathy's relationship with Nancy transformed too. There was a daily phone call from her sister to keep tabs on the progress. Soon the Monarch eclosed and they released it together, celebrating their arrival at a place of forgiveness and love.

One month later, Cathy and her husband while returning from a trip, received the sad news that her sister had passed away. It was a long ride home. They paused and sat on their porch to collect their thoughts before going inside. There, on a butterfly bush was a Monarch. Cathy, at that moment, realized that her sister was free to fly far away from her addiction.

Now Cathy lovingly raises Monarchs and educates others in memory of Nancy. What a lovely way to celebrate the special times they had shared, especially in the previous month before her death.

It's amazing how the wondrous Monarch Butterfly guided these two sisters back to each other, at the perfect moment in time. Nancy's memory lives on, each and every time Cathy releases a Monarch.

Photo Credit: Cathy Engelberger Kuczynski

October 22, 2018

Author's Note

Cathy was reading "When a Butterfly Speaks... Whispered Life Lessons", shortly after it first came out. She so graciously shared this story and allowed me to put it on my Facebook page. It just seemed to fit here and I was guided to do so. We have become friends in the process and we are sure Nancy is smiling.

October 31, 2018

I received this special e-mail from Cathy today.

"I was just telling someone about our story and I was telling her that after you wrote the story to put in your book, I had such peace and a feeling of forgiveness for my sister and my sister forgiving me. The next day you texted me and said you were going to put the story under the chapter of forgiveness. That gave me an even greater feeling... it was a message from my sister that yes, she forgives me and accepts my forgiveness as well. I am so glad we met. You have changed my life!"

Barbara J. Hacking

My response

Cathy, you have touched my heart in so many ways! Thank you for sharing your beautiful story. It reminds me of the last verse of "The Peaceful Butterfly", found in "When a Butterfly Speaks... Whispered Life Lessons".

"Butterfly, you forgive and forget.
It's the lesson we haven't mastered yet.
Because when we do, we'll have learned from you,
How to be peaceful and loving too!"

November 5, 2018

The very first Facebook message that Cathy sent me was on October 11 (10/11/2018), at 11:11 a.m. I am not surprised! Even the numbers in 2018 add up to 11. (2+0+1+8=11)

Cathy Engelberger Kuczynski

You're friends on Facebook

OCT 11, 11:11 AM

42

Time is Running Away!

August 16, 2018

While meditating, I realized that time is running away. There are signs that the Monarchs have begun to migrate back to their overwintering grounds in Mexico and soon they will be gone once again.

Last year, I saw my final Monarch on October 22, so I am reminded that although that is extremely unusual, there is still some time left with the Monarchs and there is no sense worrying about it. Nature does what it needs to do. Monarchs are no exception.

Yesterday, while picking milkweed to feed to our caterpillars, I discovered an egg. That means if the weather cooperates, there is a good month left. Hopefully, we can get caterpillars into classrooms so the students can learn from these amazing creatures.

Usually, the mother Monarch lays her eggs on the underside of the leaf where it is protected from rain and predators. Here you can see that is not always the case.

43

Monarch Magic Again!

"Above all, watch with glittering eyes the whole world around you, because the greatest secrets are always hidden in the most unlikely places. Those that don't believe in magic will never find it!"

Roald Dahl

August 16, 2018 10:00 a.m.

Yesterday was a very magical day and it looks like today is shaping up to be one too. Three stories have already been written and it doesn't appear that those will be the last.

Two days ago, I was working at Cora Couture and a lovely lady with the most beautiful red hair came into the store. She was traveling by herself from Ohio and was very interested in hearing about the Monarchs. I told her about Ted's garden and she said she was going to check it out.

Yesterday, when releasing butterflies with Aveleen and Keara, I saw this woman out of the corner of my eye. I was happy that she had made it to the garden, but unfortunately she was gone before I had a chance to speak with her. I was hoping that perhaps she would visit the store again. I had one Monarch ready to fly, so decided to take it to work with me.

Normally, I enjoy walking to work but today Mark drove me as he was going downtown anyways.

As we drove by the Court House I saw a lady with red hair. Yes, it was the lady I had hoped to see again today. Luckily, the light turned red and I

134

was able to jump out of our car safely, remembering to take the butterfly with me. Mark has learned to just go with the flow these days, as he has witnessed the miracles of the Monarchs and nothing I do, surprises him any more.

I quickly approached Marcia, and I think she was happy that I wasn't a mugger, as I went running towards her. She was thrilled to accompany me to the nearby Shakespearean Gardens to release the butterfly. She told me how her Mother had always loved butterflies and her favourite book was about them. The butterfly circled in the air around her and then rested in a tree overlooking the gorgeous gardens. Talk about coincidence! It was meant to be.

I am always amazed how the butterflies make their way to the people who need their message in miraculous ways.

44

Nana's Special Visitor

August 17, 2018

Michelle went over to visit Nana today. She was invited to sit down on the porch as Nana was expecting her daily visitor, a Monarch Butterfly!

Michelle was there to witness that the butterfly came right up on the porch, as if to say a wee hello. Apparently, this occurs at the same time every day. I'm not surprised. Barbara is an amazing soul with so much spunk and I love her Irish accent. Who wouldn't want to hang around her?

45

Transformation Takes Time

August 18, 2018

Today's date is interesting! 8/18/18

My friend, Pauline just sent me this. So true! Transformation does take time.

Beautiful transformations take time . 😊

An escapee !

Hey, that almost look like 11:11 !

Photo credit: Pauline Bokkers

46

101 Years Young

August 18, 2018 (8/18/18)

Mark and I drove to visit my Mother's best friend. On the way there I noticed the license in front of us saying 222. Mark said to check the time on my cell phone and it was 2:22. We chuckled at the coincidence.

When we arrived, Laura recognized me immediately. I had last seen her a year ago when we celebrated her 100th birthday by releasing 4 Monarchs. In one weeks time, she would be 101.

I can remember when I was a child and spent time with this spunky woman. It's nice to see that she hasn't changed. Laura still keeps a journal and plays Scrabble.

She had lived in a retirement residence for 27 years and they were changing it into a nursing home. Well, Laura wasn't ready for that, so she ended up moving several weeks ago, to a retirement home closer to her daughter.

We saw her new room and then took the butterflies out to the gazebo to release them. We invited other residents and they were intrigued by the Monarchs and had so many wonderful questions.

It quickly turned into a party as Evelyn, her daughter, had brought lemonade, cookies and fresh fruit, which seemed to multiply to serve everyone.

Laura let the butterflies go. One of them circled the gazebo and landed in a nearby tree. A couple of them stayed to entertain the residents and the rest were eager to be free.

It was an exemplary afternoon and it was a great start to Laura's birthday celebrations. Next week she will have a party and her two brothers, who are both in their nineties will be there to help her celebrate. Other family members will be there as well.

47

The Birds, the Bees and the Butterflies

August 19, 2018

I have only ever witnessed a mating pair of Monarchs here in Ontario, once in the 35+ years we have been raising Monarchs.

I thought a bat was swooping down on me. It did this several times before I realized that it was a mating pair of Monarchs. They then landed on a tree branch, still conjoined.

I have seen this many times on the Mexican Monarch mountains during the month of February. The male will fly down towards the female and when coupled, will carry her off into the air. They can stay together for many hours. Coincidentally, mating on the Mexican Mountains usually starts around Saint Valentine's Day.

My friend, Luc Picard, when he was visiting El Rosario Monarch sanctuary, had a mating pair climb all the way up his leg before they flew off. Many cameras captured this rare moment.

I find it amazing that the tiny egg the female Monarch will lay, on the underside of a milkweed leaf, will eventually turn into a butterfly. The egg is so tiny! It is no bigger than the head of a pin and is a creamy, milk colour. A female Monarch will only lay her eggs on milkweed plants as that is the only food source for her babies.

Once an egg is laid it will take 3-4 weeks for the miraculous metamorphosis to be completed.

It takes 3-5 days for the egg to hatch. When it is time to emerge, you can see a black caterpillar head dancing in the transparent shell. Eventually, it breaks the shell open and climbs out onto the leaf. It doesn't develop its stripes until a bit later. Its first meal is its' eggshell. Then it will begin to eat the leaf hairs, as an appetizer before indulging in the rest of the leaf. In fact, that's what it will continue to do for the rest of its caterpillar days, until it is approximately 3000 times its original size. Often you will see a circle shape cut out on the leaf, indicating a caterpillar has been there.

The photo in the bottom right-hand corner shows the tiny caterpillar shedding its skin for the first time. Notice that it has its stripes now and the head cap is off.

A female Monarch can lay approximately 300-500 eggs. That's a very good thing, as it is estimated that only 3 percent actually become adult butterflies.

While I was writing this, I got a text from my son-in-law that he and Rachel had found an egg along the shoreline, in their backyard and were going to raise it.

I don't know if Rachel sent this to you but we found this along our shoreline

Congrats! You have a baby to be

October 21, 2018

Serenity and I visited the Cambridge Butterfly Conservatory today, as we were missing the butterflies. I had just received my first copies of "When a Butterfly Speaks" and Serenity was excited to take her copy and read it to the butterflies.

I had a pair of mating Swallowtails fly right into my hand. Then they crawled up into my hair. They were quite happy to pose for a photo and they matched the colours on my book cover.

48

Mrs. Smith's Smarties

August 19, 2018

It's amazing how much the educational system has changed with the development of technology, in such a short period of time. When I retired six years ago, I just missed Smartboards and Wi-Fi being installed throughout the school.

I have been in and out of classrooms since then and am amazed how fast information can be found and incorporated into lessons. Although this is thrilling, we are yet to see the long term effects of this on our children, and I cautiously observe before arriving at any conclusions.

When it comes to learning about Monarchs or nature in general, technology can fill the gaps, but there is nothing like witnessing the metamorphosis with your own eyes. Seeing an egg hatch, watching a growing caterpillar eat ravishingly, becoming a chrysalis and observing a butterfly eclose, is absolutely miraculous. These events all take time and the anticipation is part of the excitement. I worry about the instant gratification our children are coming to expect.

In June, I had the pleasure of visiting Mrs. Smith's grade three class. The children had so many wonderful questions and were so well behaved; something that can be hard to do when awaiting summer holidays. Serenity, eagerly showed her class what a chrysalis looked like. We were able to use the Smartboard to show the complete life cycle, in 3 minutes!! Something that normally would take a month, but we didn't have that much time.

Blogs, such as the one Mrs. Smith creates, help keep the families informed as to what they are learning in the classroom. Perhaps the parents can learn a thing or two from their children... and when kids come home and you ask them what they did... the answer shouldn't be nothing.

Stories read by a real person, with lots of discussion, continue to be my favourite teaching tool next to hands-on learning and photos. Human connection and interaction are critical. Teachers will never be replaced by computers. I was amazed by how much information the kids had absorbed in a very short period of time.

Thanks to Mrs. Smith and all the other educators who learn with the Monarchs, for teaching your students to respect the environment and inspiring them to take care of our world.

Photo Credit: Sherrie Hearn-Smith

49

Our World is Coming Alive Once Again

August 19, 2018

This morning I was happy to see this post on the "Stratford Life" page and all the comments. People are seeing Monarchs again in Stratford, Ontario, Canada. I hope the rest of the world is seeing that, too.

Six short years ago, we found only ONE caterpillar that September and the Monarch population in the overwintering grounds in Mexico, was extremely low. We needed to open up our eyes, before they were gone forever!

Teachers going back to school this year have had no difficulty finding their own caterpillars for their classrooms. They are just buzzing with excitement and haven't needed the services of Mark, the Monarch detective.

50

Garlic Chives...A Pollinator Magnet!

August 19, 2018

When I was asked to speak at Stratford's Garlic Festival about Monarch Butterflies, I had to think about whether or not I could tie these beautiful insects in with the infamous garlic, that had created a whole Festival around it.

I said I would be delighted, as it would be a great way to discuss Monarchs and other pollinators, as well as hopefully motivate people to plant delicious garlic/garlic chives, along with milkweed. The nectar rich flowers provide food for adult Monarchs and the milkweed will feed their babies. Two excellent choices for a Pollinator garden.

It would also give me a chance to do a bit of research for my own education. My friend, Pauline, had given me a big clump of garlic chives back in the spring as hers were spreading profusely. Apparently it will do this. Deadheading the flowers will solve that problem by eliminating the production of seeds.

When preparing for my presentation, I consulted with my good friend Google. I saw pictures of Monarchs on garlic chives, as well as a chrysalis firmly planted on a stem. I was convinced that talking about pollinators and garlic went together quite nicely.

51

Monarch TV

August 19, 2018

Having two cats, Mark and I know the fun you can have watching them, watch the Monarchs. We call it Monarch TV. My friend, Olivia just had her first Monarch emerge and shared these photos of her cat, Angel, watching Monarch TV. So cute!

When I returned home, we had some Monarch TV of our own going on! Here's our Angel! (On the right).

Photo Credit: Olivia Walters (left)

Once when our cat Angel was at the vet, they were going to sedate her to get some blood work. Dr. Angela, who also happens to be my editor, opened the drawer and the first thing she saw was a box with a Monarch on it. Well, wonder of wonders when Angel saw the Monarch picture she calmed right down and no sedation was necessary.

52

Serenity's Belated Birthday

August 19, 2018

Serenity missed the nine butterflies that came out on her birthday, but had fun with her brother, Tristan this evening.

They had been traveling to the east coast of Canada, and when they arrived home, discovered that their dog had had NINE puppies.

I had been given some Swallowtail caterpillars from a gardener, whose fennel was being attacked by them. The final one had gone into its chrysalis the day Serenity returned and they were sharing my butterfly "mansion" with the Monarchs. I wasn't sure how many caterpillars I had because they were hiding in a giant pot of Italian parsley. Serenity was excited to come home, count the chrysalids and discover that there were nine.

I don't know when they will eclose, as Swallowtails are not as predictable as Monarchs. It may be soon or they might be the generation that will stay in their chrysalis until spring. If so, they will be moved to the garage for the winter as they need to experience the colder weather, like they would in nature. Wouldn't it be neat if they emerged on Serenity's baby brother's first birthday, in September? Or maybe they will wait until May, when Tristan has his birthday?? We will just have to wait and see!

Swallowtail caterpillars are often mistaken for Monarch caterpillars, yet are quite different both in colouring, shape and defense mechanisms.

Their chrysalids are also completely different, although they metamorphosize in the same way and go through the same four stages.

The best way to tell which it is, is by the host plant it is on. Monarchs only eat milkweed. Swallowtails will be found munching on dill, parsley, fennel, Queen Anne's lace, and carrot tops.

Barbara J. Hacking

You can see the Monarch's antennae but the Swallowtail only reveals theirs, when threatened.

As Serenity and Tristan explored Ted's garden, they found a Swallowtail butterfly that was enjoying the Joe Pye Weed flowers. A sign of things to come!

Oh yes, earlier in the day, we were walking along the river and espied a red dragonfly. I had never heard of a red one, until Pam discovered one shortly after the passing of Henry. They are fast and don't appear to like being photographed. I did take a video and captured two red ones; on my camera, that is.

53

Angels for Isis

August 20, 2018

Everywhere I went today, I kept seeing "angel numbers". It was just that kind of the day from beginning to end.

It was also the day Mark was taking our son Ryan's cat, Isis, to the vet to be put to sleep. She had been his best friend and her unconditional love was there for him always. I must admit Ryan is a lot like me in the way he couldn't face taking her to the vet himself.

Last night, after midnight I decided to cancel the plans I had, to be with Mark, rather than running away to avoid dealing with the situation, which is the way I usually deal with the death of a pet. I didn't actually make it to the vet's office, but planted Ice Ballet Milkweed in Ryan's garden. It's a beautiful white flowered plant and attracts all kinds of pollinators. From now on, it will be known to me as "Isis Ballet Milkweed". Isis was a beautiful Bengal kitty with interesting white markings looking like she was decorated with icing, thus her pedigree name was "Icing on the Cake".

When Mark returned, we put her in a butterfly decorated box, wrapped her in linen and tucked in cat treats, her toy mouse and a photo of our family when she lived at our house. The box was tied with a bow. She was buried in the backyard and a white Rose of Sharon bush was planted. Each August, its vanilla icing flowers will remind us of sweet Isis.

Ryan then released two tagged, migratory Monarchs. One took off towards the sun and the other rested on a nearby tree branch before doing the same. We then fondly remembered our best memories of Isis, over the eight years that Ryan had the pleasure of her company.

That evening, I released four more Monarchs at Ted's garden. I walked to the top of the bridge and saw all kinds of angel clouds. They reminded me of iced angel cookies on a blue tray. They were incredible to watch and perfectly timed! Four butterflies... four angel clouds.

These photos were taken in a 2 minute period of time.

54

One Year Ago

August 21, 2018

It's interesting, how after I witnessed all the angel clouds last night, I would be reminded of the special release one year ago which involved an angel cloud. This incredible release is described in more detail in "When a Butterfly Speaks... Whispered Life Lessons", my first book. An angel cloud appeared as Katarina released her first butterfly, in memory of her dear father.

The first butterfly I released flew into the sky that had an angel cloud in it. That release was for my father. 🦋
"Every release is a miracle" indeed Barb Hacking.
(monarch is dead center above the trees, under the angel cloud's widespread wing)

Katarina
August 21, 2017 at 8:47 PM
Full circle moment! Wow! Thank you **Barb Hacking** for inviting Jensen and I for a commemorative release of your newly hatched monarchs today - One in memory of my father, One in honour of my gift of life, One in gratitude for our medical team, and One for Frank's new health. What a feeling it is letting the air lift their wings into the sky for their very first flight. This tribute will be cherished forever. 🦋 If we don't stop to celebrate & commemorate, then we're just passing through.
"If your wings are broken, please take mine so yours can open too. 10.26.17".

There was so much for Katarina and her family to celebrate. First of all, Katarina, was the perfect match to donate a kidney to her husband. What a beautiful event to celebrate! Frank is doing extremely well today thanks to the precious gift of life his devoted wife gave him.

Barbara J. Hacking

Katarina and her mother, a few days later, were celebrating their immigration to Canada from Sweden during Canada's Confederation year, fifty years before.

A special family came to a special country… and her kidney came too! So much to celebrate!

October 26, 2018

Two Years Ago

It has been two years since Frank received his precious kidney from his gracious wife. (10/26/16) Notice how the first and last numbers add up to the middle number of 26. The number 26 refers to being selfless and serving others. I think those words sum up Katrina quite nicely.

In Katarina's words,

"When two become one. My dear Frank, if your wings are broken, please take mine so yours can open too. Happy Transplantaversary. I've already given you my heart. What's a kidney between spouses?"♥

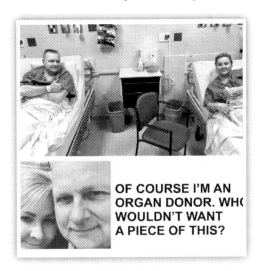

OF COURSE I'M AN ORGAN DONOR. WH(WOULDN'T WANT A PIECE OF THIS?

55

Appreciating our Elders

August 21, 2018

Olivia was excited to share her new Monarch with her Grandma, so she drove out to her farm to release it. It was so beautiful and her Grandma was excited to do it again, so we did!

How wonderful it was to see Olivia and her Grandma interact with such love and adoration for each other and create special memories together.

They had been calling for poor weather but the sun managed to poke through the clouds for most of the evening. It was dark this morning, so only one brave soul decided to eclose. That was all we needed.

56

Fall is A-Coming

August 22, 2018 (4:30 p.m.)

"We might think we are nurturing our garden, but of course it's really our garden nurturing us."

Jenny Uglow

As I sit here in Ted's garden, I am reminded that Fall will soon be among us and the beloved Monarchs that have graced this garden during their Summer holidays, will no longer be here. The newly eclosed Monarchs will soon be leaving to escape our cold Canadian Winter.

There is a breeze and the air is noticeably cooler. I'm seeing Monarchs roosting on the trees or gathering nectar from the Joe Pye Weed that towers over all of the other plants. These are sure signs that Autumn is just around the corner.

The shadows of the Monarchs dance around me as the sun comes out from behind the clouds. I look up from my writing, as I sit and enjoy this beautiful moment in nature. How I would love to take this feeling with me. Perhaps I can!

I will finish writing later as I am beckoned by the pollinators to come and enjoy the moments of the present time. No sense thinking about what is to come, or what was. The time is now!

August 22, 2018 (8:44 p.m.)

Every time I looked at my clock today, I have seen "angel numbers". It's beginning not to surprise me anymore.

I didn't have any Monarchs come out today. This was the first time in a long time! We had torrential rain and thunderstorms this morning, so I don't blame them. Later on, in the afternoon I went to sit in Ted's garden. It was strange to not take any Monarchs to release.

I saw many migratory Monarchs, so I believe I could actually tag some and set them free the next time I visit. It's so lovely to see the Monarch population doing so well.

Ted's garden today was alive with activity and inspiration, which I may have missed if I hadn't postponed my writing. I actually saw a red dragonfly. It posed so nicely compared to the ones I had seen down by the river a few days ago. It must have been meditating on the milkweed plant as it didn't fly off for a long time.

Barbara J. Hacking

I noticed that some of the Monarchs were laying on the ground. As I moved closer I could see that they were nectaring on the clover.

A tattered and torn Monarch was enjoying a snack on the Joe Pye Weed. It is one of the final Summer Monarchs that will live out its final days here in Canada.

I felt that there was a butterfly cloud peeking out from behind the trees. Gorgeous!

A Red-Spotted Purple butterfly enjoyed the beauty and sweetness of the Buddleia flower. This has always been one of my favourite butterfly-attracting plants in our garden, but the native Joe Pye Weed was the popular plant today. It was covered in bees, Monarchs and other butterflies as well.

I spotted a Viceroy butterfly (left) which looks so much like a Monarch (right), but isn't. Notice it's markings compared to the Monarch.

I had to call Mark and let him know where I was. Time had gotten away from me and I really wanted to make these moments last forever! Supper would have to wait.

> **"The more clearly we can focus our attention on the wonders and realities of the universe about us the less taste we shall have for the destruction of our race. Wonder and humility are wholesome emotions, and they do not exist side by side with a lust for destruction."**
>
> **Rachel Carson, Silent Spring**

57

Instructions for Raising Your Own Monarch

Everything You Need To Know About Raising Monarchs To Avoid a Panic Attack

August 22, 2018

Today, I had 3 amazing questions that came from 3 different people. They made me realize that caring individuals, raising Monarchs for the first time, need to know about these little tips which can eliminate panic. Having so many Monarchs around this Summer, has allowed many people to raise a caterpillar or two, as they have been much easier to find.

Instructions for Raising Your Own Monarch

1. Find a caterpillar. If it's on Milkweed, it's probably a Monarch, as the female only lays her eggs on this plant. If you see a caterpillar on dill, parsley, fennel or Queen Anne's lace, it is more than likely, a Swallowtail. (green stripes instead of yellow)

2. Feed your Monarch caterpillar the same type of Milkweed that you found it on, if possible. The bigger it gets, the more it eats, so have lots of fresh tender Milkweed leaves on hand. A mother Monarch usually only lays one egg per plant because she knows her babies will require lots of food. Caterpillars will get their water from the leaves. It is important that you don't feed them leaves that have been sprayed with pesticides.

3. The more it eats, the more frass, also known as poop, it will create. As the caterpillar grows, its frass grows too. Clean the container often. Who wants to eat in the bathroom?

4. If your caterpillar stops eating or moving, it may be shedding its skin (moulting). It is important to leave it alone and not disturb it. You may find a black blob beside it. Often it eats the skin it sheds, so there may not be any evidence that it has done so. A Monarch caterpillar grows so much, that it needs to shed its skin 5 times. The last time it sheds, it becomes the chrysalis by splitting open and removing all of its black parts.

5. The caterpillar will go on a walk-about to find a perfect place to hang upside down. It will spin a white fuzzy button to hang from, in a J-shape and its skin will split open. Its head cap, black stripes, antennae and legs will fall to the ground.

6. It is normal for the chrysalis to become black, signaling that you will soon have a butterfly. The shell becomes transparent and you can see the wings showing through. (10-14 days after becoming a chrysalis). Be sure to watch closely as you may just be lucky enough to catch the butterfly coming out (eclosing), and it is so exciting! You don't want to miss it! Many people report that they turn their back for a second, and that's when it happens!

7. The Monarch will eclose(emerge) upside down and will cling to the chrysalis. Its wings will be small, its abdomen will look like a balloon and within minutes the fluid in the abdomen will be pumped into the wings, allowing them to expand. It is very important that you do not touch the butterfly at this time. Its wings are wet and floppy and they need a few hours to dry. They can be damaged if interfered with, so make sure there is nothing in the way.

8. Have fun releasing your butterfly when the wings are dry(4-24 hours later) and the weather is appropriate. Monarchs do not fly in the rain or temperatures below approximately 13 degrees Celsius (55 degrees Fahrenheit). You will know the butterfly is ready to fly when it moves off of the chrysalis.

9. Butterflies don't usually eat for the first 24-48 hours. If you have to keep them longer, due to circumstances beyond your control, give them some nectar rich flowers such as Goldenrod, Joe Pye Weed or Dandelions or place some cut up grapes, orange slices or other juicy fruit on a flat plate. Gatorade or a honey-water solution can also be given on a sponge.

10. If you have purchased tags from Monarch Watch, make sure the wings are really dry before tagging. (www.monarchwatch.org) The tags will stick better and the wings won't get damaged.

Hopefully these tips will keep you and your caterpillar happy and stress free. The rewards of your dedication are immense, for both you and the Monarch!

58

Lincoln Brower

August 23, 2018

The other day I found a brown envelope in my mailbox. Inside the envelope was the obituary for Dr. Lincoln Brower, the 86 year old entomologist who became an icon in the Monarch butterfly world. Over the years, when reading anything about Monarchs, his name would pop up. Butterfly enthusiasts were saddened to hear of his passing. He will always be remembered for his contribution to the preservation of the Monarch species and their habitat, for over six decades.

Coincidentally, the day he passed away was the day my first book was transitioning into my second one. It is Lincoln Brower whom I dedicate this book to.

59

School Begins Soon-
Passing the Torch

August 24, 2018

I am reminded that Monarchs are still laying eggs. That means they will be around for at least another month. This is important for teachers who want to transition into their new school year with Monarch butterflies. Monarchs can bring so much excitement into the classroom.

One year, as my new class walked into the classroom for the first time, they were greeted with an eclosing Monarch. It sure got our year together off to a memorable start! It would be impossible to plan that!

I had the pleasure of meeting with Taylor today. She is beginning her career as a kindergarten teacher in a few short days and took time out of her busy schedule to learn as much as she could about raising Monarch butterflies in her new classroom. I am happy that the butterfly enclosure seen above will now be used in her classroom.

Taylor has come a long way! Last year, she could hardly look at a caterpillar. Now you can see, she has caught Monarch magic and will be able to pass it on to her lucky students.

As a teacher or parent, it is important not to pass your fears onto the children in your lives. Sometimes we need to be actors. Sometimes our children help us overcome our fears.

60

Fond Memories

August 24, 2018

I passed on my Monarch teaching materials to Taylor as she began her teaching career. It was like a trip down memory lane. How I loved having Monarchs in the classroom! If I hadn't retired a year early, I would have faced starting my final year with only one caterpillar. They were virtually nonexistent that year (at least where we live). I think sometimes we don't realize what we have until we have almost lost it.

This summer and last have been a breath of fresh air as we have seen more Monarchs flying around us, than the previous few years. I hope this is a sign of things to come and that many teachers will decide to start their year with nature in their classroom.

I came across the script of when my class, many years ago (2009) went to City Council to ask for permission to plant milkweed in our school's Monarch Way Station. Milkweed, being the only food source for the Monarch is necessary. **NO MILKWEED = NO MONARCHS.** It's as simple as that. At that time, milkweed was considered a noxious weed in our province of Ontario.

After an informative fashion show, wearing all the latest Monarch fashions at all stages of the life cycle, the kids told our city councillors about the 90 year old seeds found in a time capsule when we left our old Avon school. They asked the city councillors to think about the future kids. If we placed milkweed seeds in a time capsule, would the kids 90 years later know what they are? And if they didn't, that would mean they wouldn't be seeing Monarchs either. It was something we all needed to think about.

They then added these thoughts.

"We are hoping that the beautiful memories of the Monarch butterflies in your past will lead you to make wise decisions in the present, to preserve the future of the Monarch butterfly.

We hope that in the future our children will also have beautiful memories of Monarch butterflies in their childhood.

We can't imagine a world without them."

I had forgotten about the little play they put on. The actors included: the children, butterflies, caterpillars, Milkweed, the weed inspector and the mayor.

The butterflies tell the children why they need milkweed and the milkweed shows how it protects the eggs and caterpillars, from the rain. The children then tell the weed inspector, who is out to spray those noxious weeds, all about the Monarch butterfly and how it depends on the milkweed to survive. He in turns goes off to tell the mayor.

The story ends happily as the children are granted permission to plant milkweed in their school garden. They can now watch the caterpillars grow. The butterflies dance with joy as they will have a place to lay their eggs and have food for their babies. They thank the weed inspector (who probably talked his way into the land of the unemployed) and the mayor for protecting the Monarchs' habitat. The decision made today will protect the future.

I believe the councillors received the message loud and clear as they gave the kids a standing ovation and granted permission to plant milkweed in our school garden. As we all blew milkweed seeds around the chambers, there were big smiles on everyone's faces.

It was a tiny bit against the Ontario law, but Stratford has always been ahead of its time. Milkweed wasn't taken off the noxious weed list until 2014 and we have seen improvements in the Monarch population in Ontario. Sometimes rules are made to be broken and this is one of them.

These grade two and three students were an exceptional group to teach. They also took time out of their winter vacation to put on this Monarch presentation.

61

Symbolic Monarch Migration

August 24, 2018

Journey North (journeynorth.org) is an excellent organization which monitors the Monarch migration both in the Fall (August to November) and the Spring (February 14 to June 20). Citizen Scientists keep a close eye on what is happening near them and report it to Journey North. With the introduction of the Internet, many people can participate and much valuable data is collected and shared.

One of their projects which I had the pleasure of participating in with my students, is their Symbolic Monarch Migration. This does a fantastic job of connecting children in Mexico, the United States and Canada.

Each child in the class creates their own paper butterfly which adorns their name, where they live and the school they attend. Participating classes from Canada and the United States send their butterflies to Journey North. These butterflies are distributed to Mexican children, who will keep them safe until the spring. The butterflies will then migrate back up north in the Spring to the participating classes. It is exciting to receive a butterfly back and see where the child who made it, comes from. This is the 22nd year of the program.

Another great international project was making a quilt with squares made by children in both Canada and the United States.

At the heart of the quilt is the following saying by Baba Dioum.

> **"In the end... we will conserve only what we love; we will love only what we understand; and we will understand only what we are taught."** (1968)

Sharing in these projects helps connect children from different places with common goals; loving, living and learning with the Monarchs. It builds bridges between the countries and their people that are lucky enough to share these peaceful insects; not walls.

62

Butterflies Connect You To People You Would Otherwise Never Meet or the Stories you Would Never Hear

August 24, 2018

I was at Ted's Garden to do a butterfly release. It was a glorious morning and there were many Monarchs and other butterflies dancing among the blooming flowers. Soon there would be three more.

While I was waiting for my friends to arrive, I noticed a lady really enjoying her interaction with the butterflies. She radiated pure joy as she followed them and captured the experience with her camera. Her husband was sitting on a nearby bench admiring her, as she did so. I could tell she had found a little piece of heaven here on Earth.

The next thing I knew, we were engaged in an amazing conversation about Monarchs and Ted's garden. Bob and Carolyn were visiting from Calgary, Alberta and were on their way to the nearby Art Gallery. It didn't take long for me to find out Carolyn's story about butterflies and the deep meaning they had for her.

I invited her to do her own butterfly release, as I believe the Monarchs find their way into the hands of those who are meant to have them; often in miraculous ways.

It was a pleasure to watch her with the butterfly and have the chance to chat after. I noticed she had a butterfly ring and necklace.

Bob had given her a butterfly ring as a Promise ring many years ago. She wore it constantly and eventually it began to wear down. That ring, along with her

Mother's wedding ring had been transformed into the rings she was given to celebrate her marriage, to Bob. Of course, she had a new butterfly ring as well. It was very similar to the one my staff had given me when I retired and brought back sweet memories of the wonderful people I had the pleasure of working with.

Bob had commissioned a beautiful song as a Valentine's gift for Carolyn and it was called "Butterfly". How heartwarming it was to listen to her song of transformation into Bob's loving arms, as we sat in Ted's garden. The most perfect day got even better. It's no wonder I saw hearts and butterflies in the clouds after meeting Bob and Carolyn.

Today was also the beautiful wedding day of Monica and Jo. Monica, being an avid Monarch lover, had passed this adoration onto Jo and it seemed fitting for Monarchs to be a part of their special day. Timing Monarchs to eclose at just the right moment is easier said than done. Eleven days before the wedding, they had one caterpillar enter the chrysalis stage. It usually takes between 10 and 14 days to eclose, so time would tell whether or not it would be a part of the wedding day.

Magically, the Monarch appeared in time to be released as part of the ceremony, and the magic didn't stop there. The butterfly flew up into the air and landed on Monica's bouquet. It stayed throughout the photo session, adding such joy to the occasion before flying off. It actually landed on Jo for a few minutes before flying off to Mexico. Monarch wedding miracle?

Monica and Jo handed out Milkweed seeds as their favours so guests could help the Monarch butterflies. A nice ecological touch to their special day.

Photo Credit: Kaja Tirrul

"Never hide your wings
For without them, you would never have flown above
the past.
Always show them...
For they are the strength that you have become."

Angela C. Hood

63

The Bridge To Nowhere

August 24, 2018

The Confederation Bridge in Ted's Garden used to be a pedestrian bridge over the railway tracks. When the tracks were removed, the bridge basically became the bridge to nowhere.

When Ted asked the city to plant a Pollinator garden under it (2012), it became the Bridge to the Pollinator's future. The only thing missing was the milkweed for the Monarchs, as it was considered to be a noxious weed at the time.

The year after Ted passed away, the Ontario law was changed (2014) and milkweed was no longer considered noxious. When the four wing-shaped gardens were added in 2017, to create the Ted Blowes Memorial Pollinator Peace Garden, it became the bridge to somewhere; the bridge to all of the pollinators' future, including Monarchs. It also became a much needed Monarch Way Station registered with Monarch Watch in the United States. Its purpose is to provide habitat and food for the Monarchs during the summer season, as well as a stopping place to fuel up during the fall migration. Anyone who plants milkweed and other nectar plants can register their property. This is just one of the many ways an individual can help the Monarchs.

Lisa sent me this cute photo of her granddaughter, Serena. She had released a Monarch in memory of her Papa just over a year ago and recreated the bridge at their cottage.

Photo Credit: (top) Brilliant Images Films and
Photography, (bottom left) Lisa Metevier

64

Family Day

August 25, 2018

In all the years Mark and I have been raising Monarchs, we had never released butterflies in honour of our parents and grandparents that have passed on or for Mark's Uncle Harry who had died in WWII, at a very young age.

Today was the day! We picked up Mark's Mom and headed to the cemetery. We had enough butterflies and the weather, although threatening rain, cooperated. The butterflies were tagged with numbers reflecting their birth years and quickly flew to the surrounding trees.

We also planted some Ice Ballet Milkweed at each gravesite that appreciated the rain that appeared as soon as we were done!

65

Monarchs in England???

August 25, 2018

Mark and I are off to England soon to celebrate our 35th anniversary. I decided to Google to see if they have Monarchs in England and... the royal family came up on the screen (LOL).

August 26, 2018

When tagging Monarchs in Goderich we met a young couple from England and quizzed them on whether or not they had ever seen Monarchs in England and they said, "Never!"

August 29, 2018

Mark and I had the pleasure of exploring the gorgeous Royal Gardens in London, England. They covered a vast area and we were impressed with the number of pollinator plants (but not milkweed), adorning the gardens. We were disappointed to only see three Cabbage White butterflies in the whole garden. When we asked one of the gardeners, she said she hadn't seen many butterflies at all that summer.

We then discovered "The Secret Garden" and we fell instantly in love with it. There were so many nooks and crannies waiting for us to explore. The gardener there thought she had seen Monarchs here at one time, but not recently.

Further chatting with locals revealed that some Monarchs were seen in England, but guessed that perhaps they were blown across the ocean, thrown off course from the North American migration, by wild winds.

Barbara J. Hacking

As we walked around other parts of London, we saw one Cabbage White butterfly on a shop door, and the rest were just photos on signs and jewelry with butterflies on it.

So I guess it is safe to say, the only Monarchs found in England, are the Royal Family.

As we were waiting for the taxi to take us to the train station to go to France, this beautiful cloud appeared in the sky. It reminded me that butterflies are never too far away, in one form or another.

October 23, 2018

I just came across an article written for Journey North (www.journeynorth. org) and it said that after Hurricane Floyd hit eastern North America in 1999, a Monarch was found along England's coast. Again in 2012, a Monarch was found there in astonishingly good condition, after Hurricane Isaac.

66

Serenity's Swallowtail

August 26, 2018

I was surprised to see that Serenity's first Swallowtail butterfly was flying around the "Monarch Mansion" this morning. Serenity was accompanying us to tag Monarchs, so this was timed perfectly. Oh, so beautiful! Eight more to go!

December 18, 2018

All eight chrysalids are awaiting the arrival of Spring in our garage.

January 31, 2019

Serenity has a great eye for finding butterflies; even when it's minus 24 degrees C. outside. She found this cleverly camouflaged Swallowtail chrysalis among the hay bales.

Barbara J. Hacking

Swallowtail chrysalids hang like a hammock, by a silk-like thread created by the caterpillar before it enters the chrysalis stage. This was missing, so with the help of the Facebook page followers of "Simply Swallowtails", she was able to create a gauze replacement. When the Swallowtail emerges it will be able to hang on until its wings dry properly.

It is now safely hanging with her other 8 Swallowtails in our garage. That makes 9 for her birthday once again.

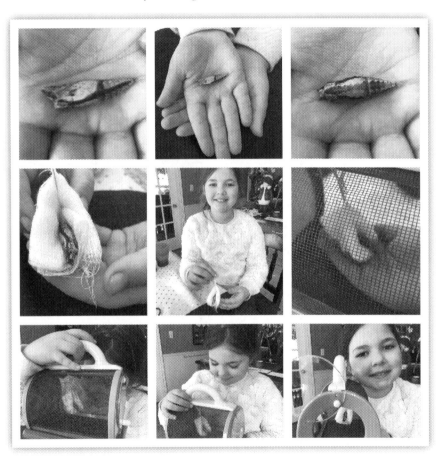

67

We're Always Learning Something New!

August 26, 2018

The sky was cloudy but the weatherman was predicting sunshine for the afternoon. Mark, Serenity and I hopped into the car to see if the social media reports, that there were roosting Monarchs in Goderich, Ontario were true…and they were!

As we drove towards Goderich, which is located along the shores of Lake Huron, after a sprinkling of tiny raindrops, the clouds lifted and the sky turned blue. With the sightings of Monarchs heading in the same direction, we were ecstatic.

We arrived at Butterfly Park, and could see Monarchs flying majestically all around us. Tears of pure joy flooded to my eyes. We had been to this park many times before, over the last few years and had seen the most beautiful playground...but no Monarchs!!!

Today, people were flocking to it to witness this phenomenon that had vanished in recent years. Social media is wonderful and we were so grateful to hear about these spectacular sightings.

We were amazed how many Monarchs there were roosting in the trees and flying around the playground. Wow! There are no words to describe this experience and do it justice.

This park is located on a cliff overlooking the gorgeous shoreline below. It truly is heaven, here on Earth. No wonder the Monarchs chose this place as one of their gathering spots before heading out on their migratory journey, away from the Canadian winter.

Barbara J. Hacking

Mark and I had never tagged Monarchs caught in the wild before and we had hit the jackpot! We couldn't wait to get started! Many people were interested in what was happening and it was the perfect time to educate them about Monarchs, their recent history and the importance of planting milkweed. The people were excited to release their own Monarch in hopes that it would be one of the ones found at the overwintering sites in Mexico.

I saw Mark's teaching skills come alive once again, after being retired for many years. Serenity learned the fine art of netting and we were all in our element! No Monarchs were hurt in the process.

Time passed quickly, and it was time for a swim in the lake and an ice cream cone.

We returned to the park in the early evening to bask in the glory of just watching the Monarch roosts. A few of them were fluttering around catching the last few rays of the day, but the majority had settled on the trees. The Monarchs had looked like fireworks flying off the trees this afternoon, but were now tucked in for the night. There would be no more activity until the sun shone brightly once again. There was a real fireworks show that evening in Stratford, so it was a little easier to tear ourselves away.

If we could bottle up the happiness we felt, we would be wealthy and it would truly change the world.

April 24, 2019

Of the 100 tagged Monarchs we released during the Fall of 2018, only 2 have been recovered thus far.

One was recovered here in Stratford, the day after it was released by reporter Gaelen Simmons. He was doing a story for our local Beacon Herald newspaper on the fabulous Monarch season we were having and it only seemed right that he set one of his own free.

Today the recovery list was released by Monarch Watch. It was exciting to see that one of Serenity's Monarchs that she released at the Butterfly Park was discovered at El Rosario Monarch Reserve in Michoacan, Mexico. It was the first Monarch she netted and released that day and it traveled at least 3,890.9 km. (2,416.7 miles) If it zigzagged rather than flying in a straight line it could be much longer. We will never know how far it had flown to buddy up with its fellow Monarchs in Goderich either. An incredible journey for such a tiny insect.

Finding a tagged Monarch is like finding a needle in a haystack if only 1 of the 100 we tagged has been found in Mexico thus far. It is still possible to find more as this generation dies and passes the baton on to their offspring to continue the migration north.

"The universe is big, it's vast and complicated, and ridiculous. And sometimes, very rarely, impossible things just happen and we call them miracles."

Steven Moffat - Dr. Who

68

Butterfly Park

August 26, 2018

Visiting the Butterfly Park in Goderich before, we weren't aware that it had been created with the help of children for a Kids' TV show called "Giver".

Back in 2012, there was a swing set and a teeter totter. A Monarch-shaped jungle gym and a tire caterpillar were added, along with picnic tables depicting the Monarch's life cycle. The transformation was perfect for one of the places where the Monarchs roost, awaiting favourable conditions to begin their journey south.

Unfortunately, that year and the year after there were very few Monarchs. How sad it would be if this park turned into a memorial for the Monarchs that used to visit here.

It was a sight for sore eyes, to see children at the park today, with Monarchs once again dancing around them.

69

Back To School

August 27, 2018

With Mark and I leaving on our trip, it was hard to say goodbye to our Monarchs, but knew they were in capable hands. My friend Mary, was getting her kindergarten classroom ready for the new school year. She kindly agreed to take the "Monarch Mansion" and look after its residents.

Now, this "Monarch Mansion" is huge and wouldn't fit into either of our vehicles. My little red wagon, from when our children were small, would become useful once again as we wheeled it to her classroom. Luckily, it was only a couple of blocks away.

People did give us some strange looks, and one car even followed us into the school's driveway. Slowly, their window opened and these two ladies said they just had to know what was in there. Of course, we were happy to give them some Monarch education in exchange for their delightful curiosity and their photograph.

My, what teachers do for their students!

70

News from Home

August 31, 2018

It was wonderful to hear from back home while we were on vacation, missing the Monarchs. My friend Elena, who had developed Monarch fever last summer with a gift of milkweed, was releasing her first tagged Monarch. She ran into other friends of mine and allowed their children to release it for her. I just love seeing Monarch magic shared.

Elena is also passing on her love of the Monarchs to her grandchildren. Lucky grandchildren!

Photo Credit: Elena Pastura

71

Pollinators in France

August 31, 2018

This morning Mark and I took the train into downtown Paris. On the way to the station we saw the cutest bee with a fuzzy white bottom, just outside of a house that was selling plants. Only one!

Then we were off to visit the Gardens of the Luxembourg Palace. The gardens were exquisite and I was in awe of their beauty. Mark and I noticed however, that we only saw one Cabbage White Butterfly. All the other pollinators were absent and it was a beautiful day. Perhaps these gardens are adored by humans, but not necessarily by the pollinators.

Later when hiking through a forest, just on the outskirts of Ville d'Avray, we saw quite a few Cabbage Whites and 3 of another kind of butterfly we had never seen before.

We approached a pond and were excited to see a blue dragonfly that seemed to be trying to get our attention. It circled around us for quite some time and I was able to videotape its presence although it was playing dodgeball with my camera the whole time.

I have now seen a red, orange, yellow and blue dragonfly this summer. Perhaps I will see a rainbow after all. My friend Pauline, had photographed a green and purple dragonfly so they are out there. Perhaps they are being seen in bigger numbers too, just like the Monarchs.

We came across the most unique pollinator house we had ever seen, on the edge of the trail around the pond. It contained many different sized spaces for lots of different insects to overwinter in. Nice to see this conservation effort taking place to protect the insects.

On the way back to our hotel, I saw my favourite number with my initials on a license plate. Then I got a message from the publisher of my first book, that it was moving on to the production stage. 111 is the number I kept seeing as I ended the writing of "When a Butterfly Speaks... Whispered Life Lessons". A terrific ending to a fabulous day of over 25,000 steps. When I went to bed, the clock said 11:11.

72

Chatting Halfway Around the World

August 31, 2018

Although I am away from the Monarchs, the Internet has kept me up to date with what is happening at home. For that, I am truly grateful!

Many Monarchs eclosed today. The Monarchs are gathering in greater numbers and are preparing for their long migration to Mexico by spending time nectaring, to gather energy reserves.

I was chatting with my friend, Pauline and she said she would say hello to the Monarchs for me. No sooner did she say that, when a Monarch landed beside her. How cool is that!

73

Monarchs in France???

September 1, 2018

If there are Monarchs in France, it would be a fluke. The only Monarchs we saw today were the ones of statues and paintings at the magnificent Palace of King Louis XIV, in Versailles, France. I have never seen anything like this place. The amount of gold within the walls of the chateau would sink a ship or feed the entire country.

The gardens were exquisite and yielded all the colours of the rainbow. We saw only a few butterflies among the massive acreage of gardens adorning the property. The choice of plants did not seem to attract nature's flying jewels. Either that or pesticides were in use, eliminating the pollinators.

One does not need extensive scientific research to know whether or not pollinators are present; just observations. It's amazing what you see when you become aware.

We did see quite a few bees on the Sedum, which grew more naturally at the sides of the path and in some of the gardens. There are definitely plants which attract pollinators more than others.

At lunch, Mark had a wasp join him. He wasn't out to hurt anyone. If you just let them be, they are quite friendly.

After not seeing many butterflies this morning, I was happy to see one on the placemat at the restaurant, where we stopped for lunch. When I took a picture of it, the time was 1:11 p.m.

While visiting one of the fountains, I noticed a dragonfly. It landed in front of us. It was grey and its wings shimmered like diamonds in the sunlight. It got me thinking back to the days of teaching all about the primary colours. When you mix all three colours of red, blue and green paint together, you get grey. Perhaps this dragonfly had all the colours of the rainbow.

A little while later, while sitting at the side of one of the fountains, I saw two flying creatures out of the corner of my eye. I thought perhaps they were butterflies so I went to explore. I couldn't believe my eyes. One was a red dragonfly and the other was a green dragonfly. A huge green dragonfly!!! I am not making this up! Mark witnessed it and I took a video, so I really was not under the influence of a dream. Again, I am learning that dragonflies like to be one step away from where the camera is. I quickly told Mark, that if I happened to see a purple dragonfly today, I would faint and he better be prepared to catch me.

In one of the other gardens, we saw a blue dragonfly. It looked like the twin of the one we saw yesterday and it was the fastest one yet. All I can see in my photos is a blur of blue.

I am amazed that dragonflies come in so many different colours and sizes. Have they always been around and I just never noticed?

Shortly thereafter, Mark told me that a butterfly had landed on my jacket that I was carrying. It was only for a second and then two butterflies circled Mark and I, before racing off into the bushes. It was as if they were playing tag. I guess I should be used to it by now, but I still get excited, as if it's the very first time.

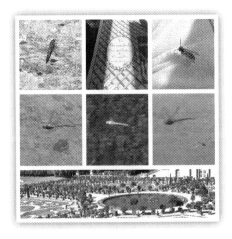

We left the grounds for supper and I saw another license plate with 111 on it. When I took out my camera, it was 5:55 p.m. Mark and I just laughed. Every time we see these repetitive numbers we just pause and see them as positive signals that we are on the right track and we share a moment filled with gratitude.

We ended the almost 35,000 step day, with an evening of waltzing fountains to beautiful music and a kaleidoscope of colour, as well as exploding fireworks in the gardens of Versailles.

While waiting for the Gardens to open for the evening, the sunset radiated the most gorgeous hues of red and orange. It entertained the massive crowd and I even got photobombed by a cute young French guy while waiting. We saw another perfect "A" cloud in the sky and thought of Allan.

It was truly a magical day in every possible way! I am grateful for this wonderful gift from Mark to celebrate our 35th wedding anniversary.

I just now noticed that's 1000 steps for every year!!! I guess if you count the 2700 steps taken shortly after midnight, we did it!

Barbara J. Hacking

September 8, 2018

Mark just reminded me that it's been a week since we visited the Palace at Versailles. This week they had to cancel the evening fountain show due to the lack of rain. We considered ourselves very lucky that we were able to engage in this once in a lifetime experience and we didn't mind a vacation without rain. A few more butterflies would have been nice.

74

Finding The Calm of the Butterfly in Paris

September 2, 2018

"Do not let the behaviour of others destroy your inner peace."

Dalai Lama

A butterfly is so calm and peaceful as it flutters from flower to flower. If only we could go through life with the calmness it models for us.

Yesterday was pretty easy to do that, as we meandered through the grounds of one of the most luxurious properties in the world.

Today however, threw us a few curves in the road where we had to remind ourselves to remain calm. It was a real test of our patience and nerves.

It was a beautiful cloudless day and perfect for walking to the train station in Chauville. We were on our way to Switzerland, a place I have dreamed about visiting since I was a child. Little did we know there would be a few obstacles in our way.

It was a Sunday of a holiday weekend, therefore no ticket booths were manned by humans and machines just aren't great for answering questions by two foreigners trying to make sense out of the train system, in Paris. A kind lady helped us at the first station and we were on our way.

At the next station, we found the platform we needed for the next train but had no ticket to get us through the turnstile. The machines were not cooperating to give us the tickets we required, so rather than stress out, we decided to take a taxi.

It was like a long maze trying to figure out how to get out of the train station, but after 35,000 steps yesterday, we could definitely manage.

We grabbed the first cab in the queue. A polite young driver helped us with our luggage and we were on our way to the main train station, once again.

It is a ride we will always remember. Our polite young driver turned into what I would describe as a stunt driver, filming a movie. He maneuvered throughout the traffic like a pro. I still can't believe we weren't crushed between the many cars in many lanes competing for a spot to get out of the traffic circle at the Arc de Triomphe. He had obviously driven in the center of Paris before and had learned a few survival strategies.

We felt like we were in the middle of a dream where bumper cars were coming at us in all directions, but never touching the vehicle we were in. It was like there was a magical shield all around us. Surprisingly we remained very calm. Mark and I just looked at each other cringing as we waited for something to happen and trusting that nothing would.

I noticed the driver, hang his finger out the window in a rude gesture when someone honked their horn at him. Well that led to a chain of reactions. A car sped up on the right-hand side of the taxi and threw something that hit our window.

Well that did it! Our driver turned into a timebomb, waiting to explode. We now felt like we were on a slalom course as the taxi sped up to the car that had used us as a target. He opened his window and threw a large two litre plastic bottle of water at the car. We felt like we were caught in the middle of a cat and mouse game.

We hoped that was the end of it, but it wasn't. We were in the midst of the roundabout, five lanes deep and our driver continued at high speed. I kept telling Mark to get his seatbelt on as this guy was out of control with his temper. Luckily for us, he was still very much in control of the vehicle we were in.

The next thing we knew, our driver cut in front of the same car and brought it to a complete halt. I don't know how a collision was avoided as our taxi stopped too, just inches (centimetres) away.

This dream was turning into a nightmare! Our driver got out of the cab in the middle of traffic and like a raging bull, darted at the other car. We could see the windows being rolled up to avoid the confrontation. Then we heard the breaking of glass before we sped off, away from the scene. We think he smashed the window with his bare hand. He came back to the car with his hand shredded in many places. Mark was looking for our box of bandages to help, but the driver needed much more than that. He knew it too, as he sped out of the traffic circle with ease and dropped us off at the side of the road. He was off to the hospital, but not before he collected his fare of 17 Euros. We had hardly moved much closer to our final destination. The meter had just kept running as we went around and around the traffic circle. With a temper like this taxi driver had, we weren't about to argue with him.

In fact, we were in shock as to what had just happened and glad to be out of the taxi alive and well. This was definitely a case of road rage of the worst kind, all triggered by the tooting of a car horn in the craziness of Paris traffic. It was definitely the most hair-raising, lucky-to-be-alive experience in our 35 years of marriage!

We felt like we were stranded, but how could that be with thousands of people around us in downtown Paris? We simply asked how to get to the nearest train station, to find our way to the main train station where we would find the train that would carry us off to the calming mountains of Switzerland.

Once we arrived at the main station we had difficulty finding humans to help us activate our Eurorail train passes. We found one but had to wait in a long line, only to find you could only get Paris tickets there.

Finally, we found the place we were looking for, tucked away in an obscure corner. As Mark walked to the ticket counter, a man behind him accidentally dropped a glass bottle of orange juice right behind him and glass shattered everywhere. More broken glass! It seemed to be the theme of the day!

The lady at the ticket booth assumed that Mark had dropped it and just left it, and she began giving Mark a hard time, in angry French. She clearly did not understand Mark's explanation. Finally, another lady took over and we got our tickets to Geneva, Switzerland. We were now off to find the calm of the butterfly. We needed to find the calm of the butterfly!

The funny thing is, someone sent me an inspirational quote this morning that basically said it was up to us to make it a great day! We couldn't help but laugh at our day, up until we headed off for Switzerland. We were doing our best to look on the bright side as we had a lot to be grateful for. We were alive and we were on our way to Switzerland, one of the most picturesque places in the world. This had been on my bucket list for as long as I could remember.

My calmness was restored as I watched the puffy white clouds in the sky outside the train window. I saw many that looked like butterflies which totally distracted me from thinking about our taxi ride in Paris.

The scenery was breathtaking and we were in awe of the beauty all around us. Our emotions went from one extreme to the other, as our calmness was restored.

When we stopped for the night in Bern, the hotel desk had a sign that said, "For service, Dial 111." We knew we were in the right spot.

The pillows and duvets were as fluffy and as white as the clouds we had seen on the train. We were definitely ready for a good night's sleep and some sweet dreams!

September 18, 2018

When I returned to work, I couldn't help but laugh at the new earrings they had brought in. They were from a company called "Escape from Paris". Their inventory number was 11 which reminded me how lucky we were to have escaped from that taxi ride in Paris, all in one piece.

Reflecting back on the experience, I laugh; especially at the question many people ask me when I tell them the story. "Why didn't you just get out of the taxi cab?"

I invite you to check out YouTube for a time-lapsed video of what is considered to be the World's worst roundabout. You will then know why.

January 19, 2019 (1/19/19)

While editing today, I noticed that the crazy taxi ride took place on 9/2/2018. The 9th month and the year numbers adding up to 11 make 911.

Perhaps it was a foreshadowing of danger. On the other hand, the month and date add up to 11, as do the numbers in the year. 11:11. Perhaps we were being divinely guided and protected. I guess it's all in the way we choose to look at it. This chapter's numbers add up to 11 as well. (7+4=11)

Even today's date has 911 among it. It also has 111. I wonder what today will bring. We are visiting one of the Canary Islands and will definitely choose our activities wisely.

When we got on the shuttle this morning, it had a sign in the front window.

We knew it was going to be a fabulous day...and it was! When I looked up 19/19/1 (today's date) I had to chuckle at the meaning. (Trustedpsychicmediums.com). "Go for it! The future is promised to no one."

Another strange thing happened today. I woke up and I immediately started to look at the numbers in Mark's birthday and mine. They added up to the same number, 43. Coincidentally, it is also the year my parents got married.

When I looked at the date we got married I saw the numbers 8,9,10 and 11. Ascending Numbers. Why I was guided to do this and what this means, I do not know but it happened at 6:11 a.m. With a 5 hour time difference it was 1:11 a.m. back home. Very strange indeed!

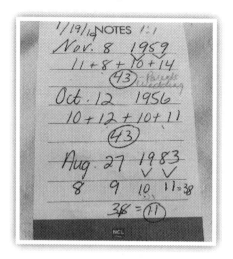

Editor's Note:

While doing a bit of research, it was discovered that there are 12 points of entry into and exit from this Arc de Triomphe traffic circle. Basically you take your life into your own hands when you enter it as the police do not investigate accidents that occur here. Each driver is considered to be at fault.

There is an underground passage for pedestrians to get to this historic landmark safely. Thank goodness!

January 20, 2019

Today, Mark and I were visiting the stunning island of Madeira, Portugal. We were absolutely in awe of its beauty. We met a lovely young man who eagerly showed us around the paradise, where he lived. I must admit memories of our horrendous taxi ride in Paris came flooding back to me. We almost didn't get into his cab, but if we had let the past haunt us, we would have missed out on one of the most delightful places in the world. As we jumped into the cab, the thought that lightning could not strike twice crossed my mind.

Barbara J. Hacking

We explored the island and as always we were on the lookout for butterflies.

A few days ago when visiting one of the Canary Islands, a Monarch followed us as we walked along the beach. It came from behind and we then excitedly followed him. Although tiny, Monarchs fly way faster than we could move. Trying to keep it in sight was next to impossible. We finally stopped at a garden featuring a Lantana bush and were disappointed that we had lost it. As we paused to catch our breath, the lonely Monarch returned and circled the Lantana bush a few times and was gone! I managed to get a blurry video and was so happy to be close to a Monarch, once again.

Mark espied the first butterfly in Madeira. It flew over a stone wall before I had a chance to see it. A few minutes later we were completely surprised when two little orange and brown butterflies danced all around us, just like when we were visiting Versailles. This time they stayed for a long time and we knew it wasn't just another coincidence. It was quite unbelievable and made us fall more in love with this magical place.

We ecstatically returned to the cruise ship marvelling at our day in Madeira. Just when we thought this day couldn't possibly get any better, we were greeted with the biggest, most beautiful rainbow arching over the island we were already enchanted with. The memories created today will be forever etched in our minds.

When traveling, we are always happy when butterflies join us. They are the highlight of any trip.

75

Other Butterfly Sightings in Europe

September 3-6, 2018

I must be missing our Monarchs as I created one, out of my breakfast croissant. I just cut it in half, opened it up and smothered it with apricot jelly. This was not intentional.

We visited Bern's botanical gardens and were pleased to see many pollinators throughout this beautiful, natural area. The native plants were providing them with an ideal habitat and they had a huge insect house, as well.

The butterflies we saw there were mostly Cabbage Whites and none were as large as the Monarchs back home.

In Bern, the Swiss capital city, they have a very old bear park dating back to 1857, housing three live brown bears. They also have free transportation and it was very easy to get there. I think Harrison, my traveling bear from my teaching days would have loved it! Bears are my second favourite animal and I think I could easily be talked into living here, if they had Monarch butterflies.

We were impressed with the planter boxes throughout the city, filled with pollinator plants. They were covered with pollinators of all kinds.

A trip to Switzerland is not complete without a visit to a chocolate shop. In Lucerne, we visited a store filled with decadent treasures. Of all the chocolates, the only ones half price were the ones shaped like butterflies. I was in my glory! Butterflies and chocolate! Prices in Switzerland are very expensive, so half the price made it even more delightful.

We had the pleasure of seeing the Lion of Lucerne and remembering that peace often comes at a price. It is a Memorial for all the Swiss soldiers that died during the French Revolution supporting the French King, Louis XIV. Little white butterflies were fluttering around the site, creating a peaceful atmosphere for those that stood and admired this amazing and moving work of art.

In Lucerne, they filled in otherwise useless areas of land with wildflowers and pollinators were plentiful and happy. People waiting for public transit were entertained by the inhabitants.

Leaving Lucerne, we saw a license plate 22222. Apparently the number two means peace and tranquillity. We certainly felt that way while in Switzerland with its beauty and charm. We weren't sure what five of them meant, but we were about to find out, as we returned to France.

The next couple of days was a series of misfortunate events. Clearly, not knowing much French proved to be to our detriment.

We got on a train going the wrong way and the first stop to turn around was an hour away with an hour wait time, in between. We didn't know that Lyon, France had two different train stations. We got off at the wrong one. Trying to get to the other one where our hotel was only 100 meters away, took us three and a half hours. We were fortunate to meet a gentleman on the train who spoke English and helped us get sorted out. He was coming back from his cancer treatment and it made our problems seem very minuscule. We also had a lovely meal while waiting to return to the correct station. We just had to get on the right train, going in the right direction at the right time and we would arrive before dark.

We got on trains we needed reservations for and we didn't have any reservations. The kind ticket man took pity on us and let us ride without charging us. We had a Eurorail pass, but didn't know there was an extra fee for the fast trains. We didn't even know there were fast trains. In Switzerland we didn't have any problems. I guess they don't have fast trains there, as you might fall off of a mountain.

We got on a train that stopped before our intended stop and had to figure out how to go further.

We learned that it wasn't the situation that life presented to us, it was our reaction to it, that either made our day a good one or not. We weren't about to allow anything to spoil this trip. Our happiness lies in our own hands.

We needed to be reminded over and over again, to find that peace and tranquility. The kind people we met along the way helped us make this time all worthwhile. We even learned to jump over a turnstile when our ticket wouldn't work in the machine. The local kids were very helpful! I bet you can just imagine two sixty year olds (plus or minus a few years) hopping over turnstiles. I must admit that we were proud that we did it quite gracefully and didn't get caught.

We had a stop in Champagne so we could turn around after boarding yet another wrong train. The station was having a power failure, so the schedule boards weren't working. Then we got some wrong advice, probably due to the language barrier. Either that, or the station workers enjoy directing foreigners in the wrong direction. This time we were proud of ourselves for discovering we were on the wrong train once again, all on our own and got off before the ticket person came around. So we were learning!

In Champagne, there wasn't very much around the station but we did come across a lovely place for lunch. With the most spectacular dessert tray ever, including authentic creme brûlée, the day was NOT a loss!!! While walking back to the train we saw lots of butterflies dancing among fields of wildflowers. Barbara, the lovely Irish woman I had met earlier in the summer, had told me the story of finding a blue butterfly in Lourdes, France. Well we found it that day and that made our errors all worthwhile. It was the only one we saw the entire trip.

Apparently, blue butterflies are rare and bring joy to those who experience its dance of happiness. It was a great reminder for us that there is joy in all situations, if we choose to find it. It is interesting that Barbara and I met just weeks before our trip and she alerted me to the blue butterflies existence.

We were on so many trains. I began to imagine the seats as butterflies. Now I knew I was missing the butterflies back home.

After two gruelling days of basically being on a train and going nowhere, we found the peace and tranquility we were looking for and desperately needed, at our last stop before going home. Our confirmation page for this place was loaded with double numbers, so I wasn't surprised. In Juilly, we stayed at a lovely 900 year old Abbey. It was challenging getting there by train but we were very near the airport and our lovely host kindly drove us there the next morning. It was such a gift to not have to get on another train. This time we would have had time constraints and we still had not completely mastered the French train system. In fact, if we had to take an exam, I'm afraid we both would have failed. A GPS would have made things so much easier!

Our room had a beautiful stone balcony and its railing was completely surrounded by pollinator flowers. We had our supper there, serenaded by the birds' melodic songs. We were entertained by the dancing bees and butterflies and breathed in the fresh country air. The overhead planes reminded us that we would be home soon.

As the sun began to set, the white fluffy clouds began to melt and cover the sky indicating that the weather was changing. From the moment we first stepped off the plane to the moment we got in the van to return to the airport we had been blessed with perfect weather. There were tiny raindrops as we left the Abbey that morning and we smiled.

Although we have had an amazing trip in so many ways, there is no place like home, where the Monarchs live!!!!

76

Secret Messages

September 7, 2018

Sometimes we receive messages in mysterious ways. I love this post belonging to Camilla Nava Soberano on her Facebook page called, "Pollinator Power".

The future Monarchs are getting ready! Munch, crunch, and munch! I'm so excited!
Oh! And maybe you can spot the love message that they sent me in the photo 😊

Her caterpillars know just how much she loves them and they are sending it right back to her! Look carefully!

77

Evan's Butterflies

September 8, 2018 (9/8/2018)

Evan Leversage, was a true light in our world. His BIG smile will never be forgotten. The legacy he has left behind continues to bring awareness and funding for childhood brain tumour research and families affected by childhood cancer. He has touched the hearts of people all over the world and continues to do so in many miraculous ways.

Evan was diagnosed with a brain tumour at the age of two. His family and the community created "Evan's Touch the Truck" event where children could do exactly that. Many vehicles are parked and children get the chance to see and touch the miraculous machines man has made. Even a helicopter has flown into the site.

This year, horses involved in Search and Rescue missions were there for the kids to see, pet and learn from.

Evan loved being a part of this annual event until he passed away at the age of 7. On September 14th, it would have been his tenth birthday.

Evan's story spread throughout the world in the Fall of 2015. The small community of St. George, Ontario, Canada rallied together to bring an early Christmas celebration to Evan and his family, as Evan wasn't expected to live to see Christmas.

In a short period of time, they pulled together a spectacular Christmas parade and a delicious feast for Evan's entire family, complete with presents. Evan was made an honorary policeman, paramedic and a firefighter which were all Evan's dreams. The whole town twinkled with Christmas lights and the rest of the world watched. A snow machine was even brought in to make this special Christmas for Evan, white.

Photo Credit: Ev Scott

The story spread like wildfire throughout the world and touched the hearts of people far and wide. It even reached Sirjit Mukherji, in India and he has created a movie entitled "Uma". It was inspired by Evan's story of how a tiny community created such joy for a dying child and his family. Evan's photo is seen on the opening screen and his legacy lives on.

Tomorrow is The 8th Evan's Touch the Truck Event. They are going to honour him with a Monarch butterfly release.

Since it would have been Evan's tenth birthday, my goal was to find ten Monarchs. Having been away for the past ten days proved to make that challenging. I just had to trust that it would all work out and we would have the butterflies we needed.

Pauline Bokkers and I headed out in the morning with a net, hoping to find some. We found lots but they were fast and got away from us or they were on the move and flying high. We finally netted one that was so enjoying a Golden Rod treat that he didn't budge. I hated to disturb it but was sure it would love to be part of this great cause. Then we found one on the road that we thought was dead but it began to move when we picked it up. That was two!

My "Monarch Mansion" was in Mary's kindergarten class so I popped in there, hoping to find some Monarchs that had newly eclosed. There were two more! Now we had four.

My daughter Rachel and her husband, Jeff were coming to visit from Orillia, which is three hours away. Jeff's niece and nephew had been raising Monarchs for the first time this year and I happened to be talking to their mother in the morning. Dina thought perhaps they would have two coming out and they did! She graciously offered to send them for Evan's Event, as their wings would be dry by the time Rachel and Jeff were leaving that evening.

I didn't want to be known as the mean lady who stole their Monarchs, but Morgan and Carter were happy that these would be tagged and be a part of Evan's special day. Perhaps they would be one of the ones found in Mexico. That made six!

Pauline, after returning from our search for Monarchs discovered she had one more Monarch that had eclosed. That made seven!

Mark had seen many Monarchs that morning surprisingly on Road 111. They were warming up on the roadside but I had the net. We returned but they had all left. It looked like we would have 7.

Now we had to wait and see if the weather cooperated.

September 9, 2018 (9/9/18)

I was up early as I was recovering from the six hour time change. When I checked the weather, it was on the coolish side but looked like it would be perfect for Evan's butterfly release at noon. No rain was in the forecast.

We were able to hand out Ice Ballet Milkweed wishes (seeds with the parachutes attached) so people could plant them in their own gardens. People commented on how many Monarchs they were seeing and they were excited! Many of the parents of the children were raising their own Monarch from a caterpillar. Having more Monarchs this year had certainly made it easier to find the caterpillars on the Milkweed plants.

There were 7 butterflies release ... Evan ... forever 7 in Heaven. They are tagged with 'Evan''s Touch the Truck'. We are hoping they get found#evanstouchthetruck when they arrive in Mexico.

Photo Credit: Ev Scott

The Monarchs were tagged and ready to go. Evan's cousins were able to each release their own butterfly so we had enough, which I felt grateful for. Erin Voss, was diagnosed with the same cancer (Glioblastoma) at the same time as Evan and her nephew released one of the butterflies, in her memory.

Evan's cousins and Erin's nephew released the monarchs in their memory. Photo Credit Pauline Bokkers #evanstouchthetruck

Gibson's Monarch decided to stick with him for quite some time before it flew away. The Monarchs seem to know when people need a little extra time with them. Gibson walked around the park totally mesmerized by his little friend until the moment came for it to fly towards the heavens, delivering Gibson's love for Evan.

When I went home, I was reading a post that Evan's Mother had put on Facebook. She had commented that although Evan's 10th Birthday was approaching, he would always be seven in her eyes. So 7 Butterflies for Evan was the way it was meant to be. Evan is forever seven in heaven!

Photo Credit: Nicole Wellwood

I just love this photo; especially the light shining upon Evan and his pal. Shortly after this photo was taken, Periwinkle was hit by a car. Exactly one month later Evan joined him.

It's coincidental that this story is number 77 and that was not planned! The two 7's add up to 14 which is Evan's birthday calendar date. Also, I finished writing it at 7:00 a.m.

To learn more about Evan and his incredible legacy, be sure to check out "Evan's Journey with Childhood Cancer. Evan's Legacy".

78

The Wonder of Childhood

September 10, 2018

The thing I miss most about teaching is the curiosity of the children and their enthusiasm to learn new things.

Photo credit: Kate Rose

Being out among nature was always where the best lessons took place.

79

Long Lost Sisters

September 10, 2018

From the moment we first met, Diane and I have felt as though we were long lost sisters. We have so much in common and feel as though we have known each other forever. Perhaps we have.

Today we were able to finally get together after a busy summer. We had so much to share and we just picked up where we left off.

I met Buttercup, her adorable dog for the first time and gave her the nickname Butterfly, as she flew around the room in her delightful cuteness.

Diane shared her amazing butterfly experiences she had shared with her grandson, Chad, as they walked the trails near her house. She had given him a butterfly kit for his birthday and I had promised to bring her a caterpillar.

Last night, I had 5 chubby caterpillars, 2 of which were hanging upside down in jays. Today I had two fresh chrysalids, two caterpillars in upside down jays and the other one had started to create its silky button. I wasn't able to move any of them. I will see Diane next week and hopefully a caterpillar will go with me.

She also told me about attending an outdoor wedding this summer and a kaleidoscope of butterflies flew over the bride and groom as they said their vows. That is true Monarch magic and a marriage blessed by butterflies.

We were leaving Diane's house and there right before us on her porch, were two butterflies made of flowers. If the sun had been out, I'm sure real ones we would have come to visit.

September 11, 2018

Mark went out to find caterpillars this afternoon and had no luck. Tonight he checked our milkweed plants and found one chubby caterpillar for Chad. It will probably be a Chrysalis by the time Diane and I connect.

80

Road 111

September 11, 2018 (9/11/2018)

(I see 111 hidden in the date.)

The day I started writing this book, I had seen the sign for Road 111 for the first time, even though I had lived in Stratford for 35 years and never noticed it before. Every time I have left Stratford, I have driven past it. Triple and quadruple numbers were popping out as me that day, left, right and center... and they have continued to do so, all summer.

When I finished my first book, "When a Butterfly Speaks... Whispered Life Lessons", I discovered there were 111 stories when I numbered them and I knew I was finished that book, although the stories have continued to flow. I wonder if this book will have 111 stories. I guess time will tell.

I don't go looking for these numbers but continue to smile when they come my way.

The other day, while trying to find Monarchs for "Evan's Touch the Truck", Mark saw many Monarchs sunning themselves on the road. This was a sight he had never seen here in Stratford, in all the years we have been observing Monarchs. When he got to the corner he noticed he was on Road 111.

While on holidays, I received this message from my dear friend, Kate. I'm beginning to wonder about that road.

Barbara J. Hacking

August 28, 2018

"Had to share this with you, as there are only a few who would believe that this is more than a coincidence.... My crazy story:We always see cardinals and think of my dad, as they were everywhere the day he died. This morning when Sophie and I were out, a cardinal flew right in front of us which spooked me and made me hit the brakes.... a minute later a transport truck went through a stop sign..... And we were on country road 111!

We were out of course, searching for caterpillars!!!"

Wow! This gives me chills every time I read it! Is it a coincidence or divine intervention? How does one prove it? It's nevertheless, amazing!

Author's Note: January 30, 2019

I am going through a second edit of this book as I keep seeing numbers hidden within the stories and this is what I see. If you look at the date of this story 8/28/2018, I can see a 911 within it. If you take the month and the date and add the individual numbers you get 18 (8+2+8 =18). Add those two digits you get 9 (1+8=9). The year digits add up to 11 (2+0+1+8 =11). The number 911 can clearly indicate danger but the 11 means divine intervention which I think must have been present, for Kate and Sophie. Just an observation on my part.

81

Chance Meeting

September 11, 2018

Today was the first day back at the store, after our Anniversary trip. I was chatting with one of my customers and somehow discovered that she lived in the house right beside the Butterfly Park in Goderich, where we had tagged Monarchs just a few short weeks ago. In fact, there were just as many Monarchs in her backyard as there were in the park. I showed her our photos and you could see her house in the background of where we were tagging in the park.

She was able to give me an update as to what had happened there while we were away. She was also gracious to take my number to call me with Monarch news.

How coincidental is that? Monarch Magic at work again!

82

Butterfly Dreams

September 12, 2018 (6:00 a.m.)

I woke up this morning and it was 4:44. My sleep patterns have not adjusted back since our trip, so I have seen a lot of early mornings. Today I went back to sleep until 6:00 and was gifted with the most beautiful, vivid dream.

I was in a store, but at the back the owner served coffee to people who appeared to be homeless. Everyone was happy. I was telling them about the magical nature of the Monarchs and they listened, intently. One of the men came up to me and wanted to give me 2 ten dollar bills to help them. I was so deeply touched but was able to tell him that money wasn't needed to enjoy the beauty of the Monarchs. They were free for everyone!

When I went outside, there were two big roosts of Monarchs on the roof. I couldn't believe it and remember distinctly that I was agitated that I didn't have my camera with me. I wanted to call Mark but didn't have my cell phone. All I could do was enjoy the moment. Then I noticed there was a tag on every single butterfly. Now I really wanted to contact Mark to bring the camera with the telephoto lens.

All of a sudden a cloud just above the roof metamorphosed into a man's face and I wondered who he could be. He was not of this world and his arms were stretched out as if he was protecting these butterflies.

I don't remember many of my dreams but this one was very clear. Was it Dr. Lincoln Brower continuing to protect the Monarchs?

Mark had gotten up before me as he tends to get up when our cat, Shadow turns on the music, on our clock-radio. He told me today it was 3:33 a.m. and I couldn't help but laugh as I told him it was 4:44 when I first awoke and looked at the clock.

83

Don't Believe Everything You Read

September 12, 2018

I went to Google to see how to spell the word "metamorphosed" in the previous story and I came across a news flash that alarmingly said Monarchs were on their way to becoming extinct. Of course, I had to read it. We were seeing more Monarchs than we had seen in a long time, here in Canada.

Basically, if this was 2012, the article would have been accurate. It painted a dismal picture of what was happening in the Monarch world at that time. They also used a single photograph of a Monarch in Mexico dating back to 2012; the year that I retired and very few Monarchs were being seen. There were a couple of comments about the article from people saying how surprised they were to have seen many this year. I believe the author must have been using information from 2012. The population fluctuates from year to year so it's important to look at current information. Perhaps the author was talking about the Monarchs on the west coast of California, this year? If so, the article would have been more accurate if it told the whole story of what was happening in the Monarch world. Eastern Monarchs were flourishing. Western Monarchs were not.

Recently when speaking to an audience, I told them how happy I was to report that Monarchs were showing a comeback this year and people were nodding that they too, have seen more. The smiles on their faces reflected this change in a positive direction. Reports are saying this could be the best migration in 25 years. How wonderful is that!

This was not always the case when presenting. I do not claim to be a public speaker or an expert in this field, but when given the chance to advocate for the pollinators, I never let it slip past me.

My presentation has become more positive during the past two summers but the message is basically the same. We need to plant more Milkweed and native pollinator plants that are rich in nectar. We also need to eliminate pesticide use and look after the environment we share with our animal friends. Spreading the word helps more people share in the effort to create the best possible environment for Monarchs and other pollinators; also, a healthy world for humans.

When I began writing my first book in February 2017, the Monarchs' population was low. There had been the ice storm on the Monarch mountains the previous March, which was not kind to an already dwindling Eastern population.

Little did I know then that there was about to be a shift. That Summer, people found Monarch eggs early and there were still some Monarchs hanging around Ontario until late October. The experts still said the population in the overwintering grounds was down 15 percent since the previous year, although many people were expecting an increase. I still maintain that when people count Monarchs, it is only a guesstimate.

There was also a kaleidoscope of Monarchs reported to be found southeast of Mexico City. Perhaps they weren't included in the count. If some of the Monarchs had moved to a spot hidden from the researchers, that could throw off the numbers too.

This Summer has been an absolute delight! Many roosts have been seen in many places. You can see Monarchs flying above the highway. It's like there has been an explosion. I love hearing the joy in people's voices as they tell of their sightings. I have received many emails from people, especially at their cottages along the Great Lakes, that they have seen great numbers this year. This is the news we have dreamed about!

I was talking to a truck driver recently, and he apologized for hitting so many in his travels. In recent history, they weren't there to hit. This is just one of the many perils Monarchs face, especially when migrating.

Barbara J. Hacking

Many families have been raising a caterpillar or two because they were there to find. This is great because it helps people connect to the Monarch butterfly. What we learn to love, we will protect.

I received a call from a former colleague Ruth, today, excitedly telling me all about her summer raising Monarch caterpillars with her grandchildren. In fact, when they went on holiday, their caterpillars traveled with them. Being creative, Ruth and her grandson built their own collapsible container that would prevent escapees and be safe for them.

Photo Credit: Ruth Sealey

84

The Metamorphosis of My First Book

September 12, 2018

Today I received an email from the publisher with the proofs for the cover and the book, "When a Butterfly Speaks... Whispered Life Lessons".

In a chrysalis, all the components of the caterpillar (minus the black body parts) are redistributed and rearranged into an entirely new form. Seeing the text and photos together for the first time brought happy tears to my eyes as it reminded me of the transformation that had taken place.

After a few more minor adjustments, the book will be able to break out from its chrysalis where it has been hiding from the world. It's beginning to feel more real. Soon the book will be free to fly! Right now butterflies are fluttering in my belly. It's kind of like sending your children off to school, away from home.

85

Returning to the Classroom

"Teaching a child not to step on a caterpillar is as valuable to the child as it is to the caterpillar."

Bradley Millar

September 13, 2018

Mark went out yesterday in search of Monarch caterpillars for classrooms. They are now getting harder to find as the migration began weeks ago. Mating Monarchs are still being spotted, so we knew they were probably out there.

Mark has a keen eye when it comes to finding Monarch caterpillars. I always say, if he can't find them, they are not there. The other night while waiting for a friend to pick him up, he spotted one climbing up our house, probably looking for just the right place to become a chrysalis.

After putting twenty kilometres (13 miles) on the car's odometer, he returned with about a dozen chubby caterpillars and one second instar, which was quite a bit tinier. It made my heart sing, for many incredible learning experiences would be created in the classrooms they visited before they escaped, to sunny Mexico.

Overnight, many of them had made their way up to the top of the container and had already begun to spin the white button they would eventually use to hang upside down. I knew I needed to get the other ones into classrooms right away.

I first visited a kindergarten class that had already released many of the Monarchs that eclosed while Mark and I were in Europe. I found the children sitting in their circle, with their teachers and they were a captive audience. One little girl wanted to know if she could touch a caterpillar and modeled how "gentle" looked for the other children. Two of the children shied away from petting it, but one tried at the end, after seeing that the other children were safe and smiling. No caterpillars were harmed in this impromptu lesson and the children's curiosity was satisfied. Now they would be able to observe the next stages of the metamorphosis in their classroom's netted container.

The children were warned about not handling caterpillars on their own, especially fuzzy ones which could give them a rash.

The children were sitting with their legs crossed and we discovered when doing so, their legs looked like butterflies. While waving goodbye, we created a butterfly wave by locking our thumbs together and wiggling our fingers.

I had another delivery to make. This was a grade three class and the students were writing about the caterpillars they already had. They were excited to receive some more. As I circulated around the room, I was impressed at the stories they were writing. They had named their caterpillars Hope and Spirit. Those would be two great things to release into this world, when they become butterflies.

I must admit, it made me miss my September teaching days. It was always an exciting time of the year as we bonded together as a class, ready to do our very best learning.

86

What You Look For, You Will Find

September 14, 2018 (6:44 a.m.)

I woke up this morning thinking about the purple dragonfly. I know it exists because my friend, Pauline saw one and took a picture of it. Mark, my biologist husband, also did some research to verify whether or not I was on a wild goose chase.

Here are all the dragonflies I have seen this summer, so far. Red, orange, yellow, green, blue and silver. You will have a chance to use your imagination since the photos are black and white.

I will continue to look for a purple one because we find what we are looking for. So look for the good in the world. It's out there!

Tonight, Serenity my young niece was sleeping over. She was laying in bed and started thinking about people who had passed away and also her sheep, Bryan. She had a tear fall onto the pillow and she thought it looked like a butterfly. She insisted that I take a picture. It was kind of dark as she only had the nightlight on. I did and she was right!

September 15, 2018

The next day Serenity was in the back seat and told me that she was bleeding. She was upset until she discovered that the blood looked like a butterfly. Of course, I was driving and wasn't able to verify her claim until we were stopped. Right again!

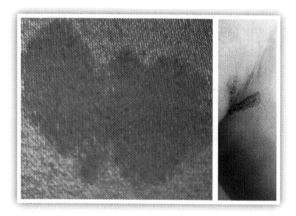

87

Rescuing Monarchs

September 14, 2018

I received a text from my friend Mary, who teaches kindergarten. One of her eclosing butterflies seemed to be struggling.

When I arrived I found a butterfly whose abdomen was stuck in the top of the chrysalis. Its wings were developing properly but the very tip of the abdomen was still attached to the shell and it was upside down . I offered it my finger and it immediately grabbed on. I was able to pull off the chrysalis shell and hopefully it will be just fine. Time will tell. I am amazed that after all these years, I still run into new situations.

October, 2018

In Macheros, Mexico, I had the pleasure of meeting Shauna and her husband. Although they live in Nebraska, we have kept in touch with the help of Facebook.

Shauna went out to shovel her driveway after a very early snowstorm. When doing so, she found a helpless Monarch trapped by this unseasonal event. She lovingly picked it up, warmed it in her hands and took it into her house, to see if it could be saved. She fondly named this female, Elsa, after the character in the movie, "Frozen".

The weather improved and so did Elsa. A few days later, Shauna was delighted to report that Elsa was on her way to Mexico once again.

88

What's Happening In The Monarch World?

Sunday, September 16, 2018

Autumn is almost here and many of the Monarchs are heading south. Hurricane Florence is hitting North and South Carolina. One wonders if that will affect the Monarchs' migration.

Mark found two more chubby caterpillars today and I read a report that someone in Toronto saw a female Monarch laying eggs, on Common Milkweed. I sure hope that is a sign of a lovely, warm Fall. Time will tell.

89

Road 111 Calls to Me

September 17, 2018

This morning I just had to stop the car on my way out of town and take pictures of the clouds. They were wispy and delicate. Against the gorgeous blue sky they looked like the artist had gone wild, with the white paint.

It was a perfect day leading up to the beginning of Autumn. As I drove back into town, Road 111 was beckoning me to explore it further. I turned and drove down the road slowly. The sky was unobstructed from buildings and wires and the clouds were even more exquisite than this morning. As I pulled over to take a look, I noticed the time on my car's clock. It was 5:55! There was a huge butterfly cloud smack dab in the middle of the painted sky! I just smiled!

90

Like Mother, Like Daughter

September 18, 2018

It was lovely to see my daughter's post this morning. This is the one Rachel and Jeff found on their own property, as an egg.

When it eclosed, Tobie, their friendly Black Lab liked her new friend.

Photo Credit: Rachel Zammit

91

Finding the Calm of the Butterfly During a Medical Emergency

September 19, 2018

Today started with a very special memory popping up on my Facebook. It's been two years since I had a very intriguing visit from a turquoise and black dragonfly, better known as Donna's Dragonfly in "When a Butterfly Speaks... Whispered Life Lessons".

I was still in bed reliving that incredible day when I heard our friend, Dave, who was putting a new roof on our house, yell up the stairs, "Mark has fallen off the roof and we have called 911!" My heart stopped! I imagined the worst and hoped for the best as I threw on some clothes and raced outside. Mark was lying on his back, on the driveway, with blood pouring from his head. The ambulance seemed to be taking forever as pressure was applied to his wound and I just kept getting him to talk to me, after he said he was "fading".

The next few hours revealed that luckily, Mark had no broken bones, but multiple scrapes, bruises and a huge gash on his head. After close observation and multiple staples to stop the bleeding, we were able to walk home. (We only live a couple of blocks from the hospital.) Mark had been lying still on a backboard and welcomed the freedom to get up and move once again. I felt like I was accompanying a mummy, with the bandages circling his head.

We noticed that Mark's hospital number had 555 in it. Apparently, it means that he is about to make BIG changes. He sure is! No more roof play! Monarchs can fly from roofs gracefully. Humans can not!

We were so grateful that things turned out okay. At the back of our house, there are three storeys. Mark fell from the garage which was one. He was able to call to our friend, who was up on the roof, for help. If he had been unconscious, who knows how long he would have been there before he was found? We are so thankful for what was, rather than what could have been.

I had to remind myself, that I needed to remain calm throughout this whole ordeal by remembering to breathe. Butterflies are excellent role models.

Coincidentally, the last time Dave was putting a new roof on our house, Mark was in a car accident. He was stopped at a stop sign and a driver behind him didn't stop. His back bumper was pushed right up to the back seat. The car was totalled but Mark luckily walked away. He hadn't had an accident since, until now.

During the afternoon I witnessed two license plates in front of me in a parking lot. One had my initials and the other had 911. Yes, I will be forever indebted to all the fine people who came to Mark's rescue yesterday. Our healthcare system is definitely a treasure in times of need. Our daughter, Rachel, who is a nurse three hours away, came to make sure her Dad was going to be okay. Ryan, our son hurried to his side as well. We discovered many blessings that day!

Our selfie looked very different from the one taken at a wedding just a few short days ago.

I went out on our front porch as the sun was setting, to bring this very eventful day to its conclusion. The clouds were absolutely amazing. What drew my attention was the cloud shaped like the 5 inch (12.5 cm) gash, on Mark's head. I went out to explore further. There was a huge dragonfly cloud. So I began and ended this unforgettable day with dragonflies.

December, 2018

While editing this chapter, I just noticed all the 9's and 1's in the date. (9/19/2018) Even the year adds up to 11... and look at the number of this chapter. Wow! We estimated the time of Mark's fall to be around 8:30, which again adds up to 11.

Barbara J. Hacking

So the 911 seems to represent danger, but the 1's signal divine intervention. All I can say is I was truly grateful that day was over and many lessons were learned.

Life can change in a second. Almost losing someone we love reminds us how precious life is and why we should never take it for granted.

February, 2019

Mark and I realized that this accident happened on Mark's late Dad's Birthday. He was born on September 19, 1927. Interesting how 1+9+2+7=19. (9/19/1927)

Mark jokingly said that his Dad probably pushed him, but I choose to believe that he was there to protect him.

> **"When you change the way you look at things, the things you look at change."**
>
> **Dr. Wayne Dyer (1941-2015)**

92

Protecting Peace

The International Day of Peace

September 21, 2018

On this day nine years ago, the school I taught at opened their Avon School Pollinator Peace Garden. We had many Monarchs to release that year! All the students at the school formed a butterfly shape and a photo was taken from the roof of the school. The children had Canadian flags which they placed in the garden, showing respect for those that served their country and those that gave their lives.

Caterpillars and chrysalids were found as the children frolicked in the warm September sun, indicating that the garden was doing what it was supposed to do. Children, gardens, butterflies and peace go together so nicely.

Photo Credit: Laf's Photography
Lori-Anne Franklin

After the ribbon cutting on this beautiful first day of Autumn, we had Mr. Stanley Turner, a war veteran, visit each class to talk about the importance of peace. He handed out Poppy pins to each child as a token of this special day. The kids were delighted to connect with him and gain a better understanding of why we should cherish peace and thank those that gave us that precious gift.

This year's theme for the United Nation's International Day of Peace is "The Right to Peace". It also marks the 70th year of the Universal Declaration of Human Rights which states that everyone, as members of the human race, is entitled to equality and freedom and ultimately peace.

Each person can do what they can to protect the rights of others and to build a peaceful world.

Releasing a butterfly on this day reminds us of freedom and peace as it goes off into the world.

Mark and I had planned to head off to Pelee Island today to see the Monarchs, but with wind and storm warnings in effect, decided to postpone our trip. It will also give Mark more time to heal from his attempt to fly from the roof.

Remembrance Day

November 11, 2018 (11/11/2018)

Today is the eleventh day of the eleventh month and the numbers making up 2018 add up to 11. More importantly, it is 100 years since the end of World War I.

Today we pay tribute to those who gave the ultimate sacrifice to ensure we live in a peaceful world. It is hard to imagine what those brave souls endured, as well as their families. They gave up so much. May we remember them and never take our peace for granted.

At the eleventh hour, during the moment of silence at the cenotaph, these words formed my thoughts, "May the peace they fought for, reign forever more over our homeland and beyond; for the ripples of war affect us all."

This afternoon, I found this photo of the rainbow of peace the young students of Avon School created as we went into the new millennium. Each student wrote their wishes for peace on a coloured butterfly. Each grade had their own colour and together a rainbow was formed. Their visions were simple, but profound. We must imagine first what we want to create in our lives. Their written words represented hope for the future.

I also read about the butterflies that the Jewish children scratched on the walls of the concentration camp, with their fingernails and pebbles. Dr. Elizabeth Kubler-Ross brought this to the world's attention when visiting Majdanek in 1946. We can only guess what those butterflies meant to these children. Perhaps they too envisioned a world as peaceful as a butterfly, where we all have the freedom to fly. The butterfly symbol represents hope.

Barbara J. Hacking

Dr. Kubler-Ross, after working with grieving souls for many years thought perhaps the butterflies symbolized the transformation that comes with death; from the confines of the chrysalis to the freedom and beauty of the butterfly.

A year ago, on Remembrance Day, this cloud hovered above the highway. It reminded me of a Peace dove or an angel. It was huge and hard to miss.

93

The First Day of Autumn

September 22, 2018

Today is the official first day of Autumn. I am reminded that our Monarchs will soon be gone. I visited Ted's garden a few times this week and have not seen any. Although it somewhat saddens me, I am happy that they are on their way before the colder weather sets in. Yesterday, we were surrounded with strong winds which hopefully helped them on their way rather than hindered them.

There are reports from our American friends, that they are seeing huge numbers of Monarchs migrating and everyone is ecstatic and optimistic that things have turned around for these amazing insects. The weather conditions have helped them this summer and hopefully will continue to be favourable. People are planting milkweed and nectar plants which provide valuable nourishment and habitat. We can only hope that things will continue to move in the right direction.

I still have eleven chrysalids that will eclose soon. They were caterpillars that Mark discovered when we returned home from traveling. They had hurried into their chrysalids before I was able to get them into classrooms.

Barbara J. Hacking

I must admit I love having them close! The last caterpillar formed its chrysalis yesterday.

Mother Nature has started her yearly painting session and the trees are looking amazing, as they glow in the sunlight. The leaves fall from the trees and spin in the breeze; they trick me into thinking they're butterflies dancing through the air.

I am filled with so much gratitude for this awesome Summer. The Monarchs were here early and people are noticing their emergence. Large numbers have been witnessed all over Ontario, especially along the shorelines. Some scientists say this is the best season in twenty-five years! I look forward to visiting the magical, Monarch mountains in February.

People who tag Monarchs have run out of tags because there were way more Monarchs than they ever imagined possible in their wildest dreams, based on their experience in recent years.

Just a few short years ago, Mark and I saw 14 Monarchs all summer and we were on the hunt for them. We traveled far and wide to places we had seen them before and were severely disappointed. The ones we did see were in pollinator-friendly gardens including milkweed, emphasizing the need for proper habitat creation. People are more aware and want to help so they keep this in mind, when selecting native plants.

Autumn is such a beautiful time of the year! I have already started to miss the Monarchs, although there are still some here.

This Autumn angel cloud appeared in the sky today. Just one of the many miracles this time of the year brings, to those who wish to see.

94

A Glorious Day at Pelee Island

September 23, 2018

Mark and I enjoy visiting Point Pelee National Park which is located at the most southern spot in Canada. This year we decided to go to nearby Pelee Island as we had never been there before. It was a beautiful, sunny Autumn day and perfect for the ferry ride over.

When we exited the ship, we were greeted by a large Monarch flying above our heads. We hoped that was a sign of what we were going to see on the Island.

Our friend, Luc Picard was camping there and was graciously ready to show us around. Our first stop was the beautiful garden at the Pelee Island Winery. The Zinnias were amazing and all kinds of pollinators were enjoying their sweet nectar. We only saw a few Monarchs but many other butterflies were fluttering around. Mark was able to find one half-grown caterpillar. It was left there and hopefully the weather will cooperate so that it gets to join the Monarch migration.

After lunch we returned to the garden, with a net. We were only able to capture and tag one. We guessed that the Monarchs were well on their way to Mexico.

The highlight of our visit was seeing a White-striped Sphinx Moth dancing among the Zinnias. It really did not seem camera shy and entertained us for quite awhile. It made the trip all worthwhile.

The last ferry of the day was at 4:00 p.m., so we were on our way. It was a day to remember. We could see why the Monarchs choose Point Pelee and Pelee Island as their stepping stones to the United States(Ohio). From the ferry we could see all three locations. Monarchs are so incredibly smart! Or programmed? Or magical?

95

Christi's Butterfly

September 24, 2018

My good friend Christi, retired from her grade one classroom in June. After being dedicated to the many students whose lives she touched in such a kind and caring way, she was now free to find her life on the other side of the school door.

There is no better way to leave behind the career you loved than with a butterfly release. We had visited a kindergarten class in the morning, shared our Monarch experiences with a new teacher and were confident that the children were in excellent hands. Christi was ready to set her butterfly free.

Christi also recalled that it was twenty-five years since her dear Mother had passed away, at a very young age. Christi, one of ten children, was just a new Mother herself at the time and she missed her terribly, even after all these years.

This female butterfly would do double duty. She was one of the final butterflies we would see this season and Christi was happy to send her off on her long journey.

The Monarch decided it needed to crawl up Christi's face and give her butterfly kisses on her neck before taking off. It circled several times and then off it went, high into the sky. She was off to Mexico!

Christi took some Milkweed seeds that were ready to travel to a new location and set them free; perhaps making a few wishes for the future.

Barbara J. Hacking

Christi celebrated her dear Mother with a butter tart complete with raisins; just one of many special memories that she holds dear to her heart.

Christi and I have been friends since our early teaching days. We had our children at the same time and I am looking forward to spending more time with my valued friend.

96

Flashback

September 24, 2018

I love when Facebook sends memories from the past. I adore these photos of Lincoln and Pearl from four years ago. They had played hooky from school to release my last Monarch that year! My how they have grown!!! I'm glad their mother Morgan, recognized how precious time spent with your children is.

Looking back, helps us remember what matters the most.

97

Pollinator Summit

September 25, 2018

Today, the Bee Cities of Ontario gathered together for the Pollinator Summit. There are many dedicated citizens of the Earth who want to help now to correct the damage humans have done in the past, so that the future is bright for mankind.

The Summit was opened by Kim Wheatley, an Anishinaabe cultural consultant. Her message was very touching and clear.

She reminded us that everybody is responsible for taking care of the flora and fauna and that one day we will return to the Earth. The children who are yet to come, deserve a world even better than when we first arrived and we need to make changes, if that is to be. In order to protect nature we must really feel it in our hearts. We need to reconcile relationships among the planet.

Kim's words were delivered with great hope, love and respect and she invited us to take what we were about to learn as a gift and share it with the world.

Photo Credit: Kim Wheatley

98

The Miraculous Migration

September 25, 2018

I received a message recently from a concerned person who had seen Monarchs washed up on the shores of Lake Ontario. It reminds us of the miraculous nature of their migration. What they endure on their trip is amazing, considering the Monarchs weigh less than a small paperclip.

My response was, "Nature can be cruel. They are very smart and usually know how to move at the best possible times. I would say that they misjudged or Autumn winds overpowered them. The Monarchs have had an amazing summer, so hopefully this will not set the population back."

My friend Luc, carries a paperclip in his pocket as a reminder of their fragility. They weigh the same. I am constantly in awe of this little insect!

99

Monarch Wishes/Butterfly Kisses

September 25, 2018

Photo credit: Cathy Engelberger Kuczynski

Each milkweed seed is a wish for the Monarchs, perfectly packaged by Mother Nature. The brisk Autumn winds will carry each seed to its final resting place. If the conditions are right, it will grow into habitat and food for future Monarchs.

October 14, 2018

Today was sun-kissed! A gentle Autumn breeze was coaxing the milkweed seeds ever so slightly to escape from their pods. Once set in motion, looking like musical notes, they freely dance through the air to who knows where. What does their future hold?

December 22, 2018

Butterfly kisses are when you flutter your eyelashes affectionately on someone's cheek. Judy Guptill gives a new meaning to this term.

Judy posted this amazing idea on Facebook. She was making seed balls which can be used for planting milkweed, in hard to reach places and creatively came up with the idea of "Butterfly Kisses" Monarch-style.

Barbara J. Hacking

Photo Credit: Judy Guptill

Here is Judy's recipe for Seed Balls.

Materials: 1 part milkweed seeds
              2 parts potting soil
              2 parts air-dry modelling clay

Method: Mix the materials together. Form it into the desired shape with a milkweed seed fluff sticking out of the top. Let them air-dry for about 3 days.

The "Butterfly Kisses" can be tossed, in the Fall. This allows them to experience a cold period before they germinate in the Spring. If you want to toss them in the Spring, then the seeds can be placed in a cold place such as a garage or shed for the Winter months.

The seed balls will soften with moisture from snow or rain and the seeds will grow when the conditions are ideal.

Butterfly Kisses help the Monarchs by producing new milkweed plants. Judy also helps the Monarchs by collecting seeds from native milkweed plants and sending them by mail to people willing to plant them to create habitat and food for them. It's a lovely gesture on her part to make this world a better place.

100

Ryder's Butterfly and Rainbow Ruby

September 26, 2018

The Monarch that eclosed yesterday was quite tiny. It had emerged from a smaller than usual chrysalis but was perfect in every way. The Monarchs that are migrating are usually larger and brighter in colour.

Two year old Ryder wasn't sure he wanted to see it at first. When his mother, Sheila modeled her delight, he quickly became involved in the release.

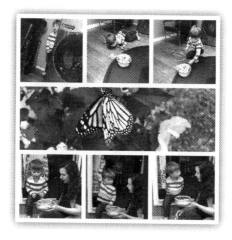

As Ryder prepares for the addition of his new baby sister to the family in early November, I am reminded that the Monarchs will be entering Mexico at that time. Will this tiny one make it to Mexico?

Barbara J. Hacking

November 1, 2018

Little Ruby Marie arrived just in time for the Mexican celebration of Dia de Los Muertos. Her birth is certainly something to celebrate too as she is a treasured rainbow baby. After holding this precious wee one, I can say she is perfect in every way, just like the Monarch her brother released while awaiting her arrival. Ruby is bringing much joy to her family.

Photo Credit: Joanna Lynn Photography (bottom right)

It is only lately that I have begun to hear the term "rainbow baby". It refers to a child born after the loss of a child.

*Author's Note

January 11, 2019 (1/11/19)

While editing my photos today for this book, I discovered that the numbers surrounding Ruby's birth were very mystical and full of 1's. Even today's date has a 1111 within it. I am becoming fascinated with numbers and am quite amazed how they pop out at me, since I began to write this book.

Ruby's birth date is full of ones. 11/1/2018. The year adds up to 11 too.

If you add the numbers of the time she was born you also get 11. (8+3+0=11)

Her weight numbers add up to 19, which is also her length. If you add 19+19 you get 38. Add these two numbers together and you get 11.

Even this chapter's numbers add up to 1. (1+0+0=1) You can't say that for any chapter other than the first and tenth.

What are the odds that on this date, I would look at the above photo and see all the 1's? Intriguing!

This is a photo that was taken shortly after this story was edited. It looks like there is a butterfly light at the top of the rainbow.

101

I See Butterflies Everywhere!

September 27, 2018

Yesterday, while picking my friend Carys up to go to Edmonton, Alberta we saw a canary yellow butterfly camouflaged against a dandelion flower. Dandelions bloom early in the Spring and their sweet nectar serves as food for the pollinators. They bloom again in the Fall, if left to grow and become one of their last nectar sources.

When we arrived at our hotel, the welcome sign for the National Communities in Bloom Symposium had a similar butterfly. That was just the beginning of seeing butterflies in unusual places.

It was very late and I thought I was imagining things when I noticed the fire alarm light looked like a silver butterfly. I just laughed. I must be deliriously tired!

In the morning, it still looked the same. The face cloths in the bathroom also looked like a butterfly.

I guess what you focus your attention on, multiplies.

102

Monarchs in Alberta???

September 28, 2018

Today, as part of the National Communities in Bloom Symposium, we visited the Muttart Conservatory in Edmonton. What gorgeous plants! The only thing they were missing were the pollinators. It made me think of what it would be like without them in our world.

In one of the four glass pyramids they had the most beautiful display of Mexico and its upcoming celebration, Dia De Los Muertos. It is a day where many people in Mexico honour their family members who have died and create altars to celebrate their lives.

A long time ago, the Mexican people would see the Monarch butterflies migrating in large numbers around the beginning of November and they believed they were the souls of their dead ancestors. The only thing missing from this beautiful display were the Monarchs.

We also visited the John Janzen Nature Area. Looking at their pollinator plants, I felt like I was in a different world. I guess I was, as Edmonton is over 3,000 kilometres (1800 miles) away from Stratford, Ontario. Their native plants were very different from ours and there was no milkweed.

The guide said that their main butterflies were Painted Ladies and everyone I've asked this summer from Alberta, knows of the famous Monarch but really wasn't sure whether or not they had seen them in their province…but then again, up until last summer we hadn't seen many either. They were however, selling Monarch wings in their gift shop.

Barbara J. Hacking

The Nature Area had a wonderful bee display and even a huge climber for children, looking like a bee hive. In the garden they had an insect house containing many different tubules for different sized insects to overwinter in.

103

Meanwhile Back Home

September 29, 2018

Three of our remaining chrysalids had eclosed and the Monarchs were ready to fly. The weather cooperated, so wearing their migratory tags they were off, thanks to Mark!

104

Signing the Final Papers

September 29, 2018

While preparing for the Awards Ceremony for the Communities in Bloom Symposium, I received a phone call from Balboa Press. It came at just the right time as I actually had some time to finalize my first book, so it could go off to the printers.

There were some minor changes needed on the cover. They quickly made the corrections and sent them to me. There was an 888 on both versions so I was pretty sure they would be perfect and they were.

My project number was 783397. I noticed that the email, with the sign off form, was at 3:38.

They then wanted me to send the preview of my book that would be available to potential readers and my selection were pages 33-38 from the book. Very uncanny! I had chosen the selection months ago, without knowing what the page numbers would be.

*Author's Note: I can see a 911 when adding the 9th month and the numbers in the date. (2+9=11) It makes me thankful we weren't flying home that day!

105

Reflecting on the Symposium

September 30, 2018

Traveling home from Edmonton gave me lots of time to think about what I was taking away from the Symposium. Seeing many beautiful photos of the Communities not only in Canada, but throughout the world, filled me with gratitude for gardens and the beauty they add to the Earth.

What are gardens without pollinators? We must continue to reflect on our gardening practices and plant native plants suitable for native pollinators. This summer I have seen many gorgeous gardens, void of pollinators. Their absence is sending us a strong message.

If you plant for them, they will come! If you spray the plants, they won't.

106

Serenity's Butterfly

October 1, 2018

It was a rainy, cool day; a sample of days to come, I'm sure.

When Serenity came home from school she was so excited to see that her Monarch had eclosed and it was a boy! She quickly called to see what to do as the weather was not conducive for a release. Rain is predicted for tomorrow but hopefully there will be a break in the weather to get this fellow on his way to Mexico. This time of the year it's Monarchs against the weather.

October 3, 2018

Yesterday was rainy and cool. Certainly not an ideal day to release a butterfly. Today was warmer and Serenity helped her little brother Tommy, release his first butterfly. He had just turned one!

107

Flashback

October 2, 2018

I woke up this morning thinking about the dragonflies that had shown up in my life this summer.

Earlier in the summer, I was asked to come and help a dragonfly that had been flying around the store window, where I work. My co-worker, Lesley rescued it and put it outside on a planter. She was worried that the busy street may not be a very safe place for it.

Serenity and I put it in a container and walked it down to the Shakespearean Gardens. As soon as we went through the archway of the garden, we saw a dragonfly exactly the same. Black and clear wings dashed among the flowers. We were sure this was the best place to release it as it would have a friend.

Unfortunately when we put our new friend on the flowers it had passed away. We were sad. Little did I know then that this was the preview of a summer with mysterious dragonfly sightings.

Barbara J. Hacking

*Author's Note

Apparently a female dragonfly will pretend she is dead if she doesn't want a male to come after her. Perhaps she was feigning her death.

Going back even earlier in the Spring, I was on a hike through Hulett Marsh with my friends, Pauline and Angela. It was too early for the Monarchs but we saw many dragonflies just waking up after a long winter. They were everywhere and looked gorgeous as they basked in the warm, Spring sunlight.

The first one we saw was shimmering in metallic gold. The others were black and white. None of them displayed the rainbow colours I was to see as I traveled through the days of Summer. Very strange! In fact, even in my wildest dreams, I wouldn't have believed dragonflies even existed in all the rainbow colours.

They were a lot slower and much easier to photograph! I guess these Spring visitors were also a foreshadowing of things to come.

Pauline even had a friendly visit from one.

When I was preparing the photos for this book, I noticed that the gold dragonfly had a black butterfly shape hiding on its wings. Can you see it?

Perhaps all insects are making a comeback!

October 8, 2018

Pauline sent me one of her photos from our hike at the Hulett Marsh. One of her photos showed a black and clear winged dragonfly, with a purplish tinge. So they do exist!

108

Awakening

October 2, 2018

As the Monarchs return and grace our world with their presence, may we hear the silent messages they bring.

What a refreshing Summer it was, with perfect weather for the Monarchs. People were excited to be noticing that they were here. Last summer was just a taste that we were moving in the right direction but this Summer there was a colossal explosion. They were here early and there are reports that there are still some here.

It was great to hear the excitement in people's voices as they rejoiced in the emergence of what was once, almost gone.

We must continue to plant Milkweed to provide a habitat and nourishment for their caterpillars. Native nectar plants attract and feed lots of different pollinators, as well as adult Monarchs. Natural gardens without the use of pesticides are critical to ensure a healthy, pollinator population.

Environmentally sound practices must be taught and followed in order to make our planet not only healthy for pollinators but for all animals and ourselves. Future generations deserve healthy surroundings.

What we do for pollinators, we do for all animals.
What we do for the animals, we do for mankind.
What we do for mankind, we do for our children.
What we do for our children, we do for their future.

Our final chrysalis should be eclosing any day now. It signals the end of Monarch season for us. Hopefully the weather will cooperate and it will make it safely to Mexico.

109

Monarch Visitor

October 2, 2018

Rachel and Jeff were out hiking this evening and a Monarch appeared. It was warming itself on the road. They picked it up carefully to make sure it wasn't injured. It was fine and flew off to a tree for the night. Tomorrow is supposed to be warmer and hopefully it will be on his way to Mexico.

Rachel usually sees Blue Herons. Today she encountered a Monarch and I witnessed a Blue Heron along the river, while walking home. As I grabbed my camera, it flew off majestically. I just enjoyed the moment.

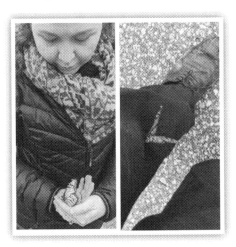

110

Butterfly Blessings

October 3, 2018

As Monarch season winds down here, I am reminded of the many blessings they have brought to me throughout my life, especially this summer. I am grateful for the people I have met, their willingness to share their stories and all the miracles/coincidences/synchronicities that have occurred. It truly has been a magical Summer and I have continued to learn many lessons.

I came across a Facebook article today that reminded me of just how far the Monarch population has come in a short period of time. In 2016, the Committee on the Status of Endangered Wildlife in Canada had discussed declaring Monarchs as Endangered instead of a Species of Special Concern. (www.registrelep-sararegistry.gc.ca)

It will be interesting to see what happens this year, after a booming summer.

David, a guide at one of the Monarch sanctuaries in Mexico was posting how excited he was that the Monarchs would soon be back and he was preparing for their arrival. He promised to keep us updated on Facebook as to what's happening on the Monarch mountains this winter. All being well, it should be spectacular! That certainly makes the end of the season here much more bearable.

I was able to share with him that I still had one chrysalis and that I would be sending the butterfly within, on his way soon. Perhaps David will be the one who finds it!?

How lovely it is, that the North American countries have the luxury of sharing this amazing insect and are connected by its wondrous migration... and the internet.

111

An Extraordinary Ending to This Book (Believe It Or Not)

October 4, 2018

I was pretty certain that this book would contain 111 stories, just like my first book. (That had not been planned!). As the day progressed, I was sensing that I was being directed to end this book as the Monarch season here was drawing to a close, concentrate on the marketing of my first book which would be out any day now and move on to book number three.

I was off to visit my daughter, Rachel who lives three hours away. It was a glorious sunny day and after many cloudy, rainy days it felt exhilarating to be driving through Mother Nature's glowing art studio. It was as if the trees had become her canvas and she was using her palette of blissful golds, oranges and reds. How I love this time of the year when we are thankful for these gifts of Autumn treasures and the precious time spent with our families!

I had a lot of thoughts traveling through my mind and it came to me that the name of this book needed to change from "When a Butterfly Speaks... More Whispered Life Lessons" to "When a Butterfly Speaks 2... Celebrating the Return of the Silent Messengers". After all, it was the perfect Monarch Summer. The weather was ideal for creating a generous Monarch population. With their return, came these stories.

I decided that I needed to stop the car and write it down before I forgot. That's when I looked up and noticed the house sign in front of me. The last three numbers were 777. Again, I took that as a sign that I was listening to and hearing divine guidance. Then I happened to look at my dashboard. The time was 11:11 and the temperature was 11 degrees C. There was even a bright beam of the sun's rays, acting as a spotlight between the time and the temperature, ensuring that I didn't miss seeing these repeating numbers. One minute later it would have vanished. Wow!

When I returned to the road, I couldn't believe what had just happened, but I was convinced that the name change was the correct decision. Little did I know that was just the beginning of having numbers jump out at me, for the rest of the day.

As I got closer to my daughters house, I began to see a series of numbers containing 1's and 3's. It seemed as though they were trying to get my attention. As I drove on Highway 11, I passed Oro Roads 11 and 13. I began to take notice of what was going on. A truck passed me and had its phone number on the side, ending with 3333. I stopped at a roadside corn stand. They had a sign at the end of the driveway that had an 11 on it and the time was 1:03 and it was 13 degrees C. As I moved closer to my turnoff, the Orillia sign said the population was 31,000. I just smiled. Just then the GPS told me to turn off at 131A. When I did that, I had to pull over to take a photo of the time. It was 1:13 and it was 13 degrees C. The numbers were certainly entertaining and made the trip one to remember.

Barbara J. Hacking

When I met up with Rachel for lunch, I couldn't wait to tell her about my morning. Before we even got out of the parking lot, a car with 313 on the license plate drove by and the number on the ticket machine began with a 1 and a 3.

I decided to buy a lottery ticket, which I never do but it was for 60 Million dollars. I thought of all the pollinator gardens I could put in with that kind of money. (Even the time at the top of the ticket was loaded with 1's and 3's. 01:31:03! I didn't notice that until I checked the ticket to see if I had won anything.)

I decided to use my family's birthday numbers and guess what? They were all selected. So I ended up getting 4 out of the 7 which I thought was amazing, however it only resulted in a win of $20.00. I don't usually win anything so I was pretty excited! The double numbers that I had also picked, like 11 and 33, didn't come up at all and reminded me that family was more important than the money I would have won, if these numbers had been selected.

After spending a lovely afternoon having lunch with Rachel and Jeff, at the Mariposa Market (Mariposa means butterfly in Spanish) and shopping, I returned to my car. There was a taxicab waiting for a passenger right beside where I had parked and I couldn't help but notice his telephone number. It ended with 3333. The driver was outside of the car and smiled when I told him I loved his phone number. It was like he was just standing there waiting for me to arrive so he could show it off. When I got in the car, the time on the dash was 5:33 and the temperature was 11 degrees C.

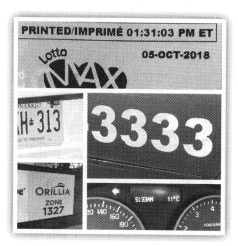

Oh my! I'm sure Jeff thinks that his mother-in-law has gone off her rocker and perhaps you do too! All I can say is that Story 111 sure lived up to its name! I think the message was clear that I was to move on to Book 3.

Bedtime tonight! 11:11 p.m.

My good friend, Mary Ford-Pleil, enlightened me to the fact that 11:11 is the only time on the clock where you will see all four numbers the same. You will only see it 2 minutes per day, out of a possible 1440 minutes!!!

October 11, 2018

As I was editing photos I discovered I had taken this photo on October 1st. Perhaps it was a foreshadowing of things to come?? It was a rainy day and I noticed this license plate. For some reason I actually followed the truck into a drive through, to snap this photo. Very strange… but is it? The date (10/1/2018) creates 11:11 when you add the month and the date together and then the numbers in 2018. Even today's date, has 11111 hidden among it. (10/11/2+0+1+8).

You can also create a lot of 36's from the numbers on the license plate. You will hear more about that, in Ending Number 3.

*Author's Note

This book truly did not want to end, therefore I wrote what I thought was the ending many times. From Canadian Thanksgiving in October until February 22, the words kept flowing and all I could do was write them down. I decided that perhaps people would like to choose their own ending.

Here are a few guidelines.

Ending Number One

If you would enjoy an ending filled with gratitude, this is the ending for you. Also, if you are curious about whether or not the purple dragonfly ever showed up.

Ending Number Two

If you agree that many of the events with the butterflies in this book, are mystical.

Ending Number Three

If you were a friend or family member of Ted Blowes or have an interest in numerology, especially the number 36.

Ending Number Four

If you enjoyed the ending of "When a Butterfly Speaks... Whispered Life Lessons", this one is similar.

Ending Number Five

If Halloween is your favourite holiday, these crazy skeletons will give you a good laugh from beyond the grave.

Ending Number Six

Barbara J. Hacking

If you are Mexican or enjoy learning about special celebrations from around the world. Dia de Los Muertos is celebrated on November 1, each year. The Mexicans would see the streams of returning Monarchs and believed they were the spirits of their family members who have gone before them.

Ending Number Seven

If you are a true Monarch-lover and are wondering how this year's migration went, or planted milkweed and nectar plants and want to know if your efforts are helping.

Ending Number Eight

If you believe in Christmas miracles, this is the ending for you. Even if you don't, perhaps you will.

Be sure to check out my "Author's Final Note". It also seemed to keep on growing.

The Monarchs are Leaving! Now What?

1

The Ending... Or So I Thought!

October 5, 2018 (a. m.)

Our Canadian Thanksgiving weekend is here. I am so grateful for the butterfly experiences that have come my way. The stories have flowed onto the pages of these two books. Never have I had writer's block. I guess it's really true that you never have to force anything, that is truly meant to be. It was as if the metamorphosis of the Monarch population from a "Species of Special Concern" over the last 21 months, coincided with the metamorphosis of these stories. It is in fact, the increasing population of the Monarchs that created them. If the declining population had remained, these books would not even exist.

My first book, "When a Butterfly Speaks... Whispered Life Lessons" did not want to stop being written. It was such a struggle! Not to write, but to stop. Now I know why; the Monarch story was not yet complete. Perhaps it isn't now, either. All the 3's I saw yesterday, might just be a hint that a third book is on its way. Time will tell. Time will also tell if the Monarch population will continue to grow in the right direction and whether the numbers in Mexico increase this Winter. We as humans must explore what is happening to change this once devastating situation around and keep on doing what is working.

I used to wonder where these stories came from. All I know is that they have come through me but not from me and why, it matters not. Perhaps in time I will figure that out. I am grateful for these stories and the people and experiences that created them.

I do not claim that double and triple and even quadruple numbers have any meaning; I just know they show up often and make me pay attention. They remind me to smile and show gratitude each and every time I see one, for

Barbara J. Hacking

I have so much to be thankful for. It seems that the more I pay attention, the more there is to pay attention to.

I no longer worry what people may think as these stories go off into the world. I am not going crazy, as I once thought. I have been blessed in ways not understood by the human mind. The word miracle has become an everyday occurrence. Now if I told you that I was making all of this up, I bet you would believe me. I'm just happy that my phone documents each moment (the place, the date, the time), if I can get it out in time and if I'm not driving.

I was once doing a presentation where I had said, "... and I have photos to prove it." A wise lady came up after and said that I didn't need to prove anything to anybody. She was a retired Crown Attorney and I appreciated her advice. (Don't they usually need proof for everything in the court system?) Her wise words come back to me often. She had seen many butterflies since the death of her mother and didn't need convincing that there is something magical about them.

I am grateful to those people who have allowed me to orally tell them about these stories while writing this book. If I had kept them to myself I think I would have exploded.

The more I wrote, the faster the stories came. This summer has been amazing! It's like the world was awakening as the Monarchs graced our land once again, along with all the other pollinators.

Now, about my search for the purple dragonfly. Sometimes we find what we are looking for in unexpected places. You may recall, that Mark fell off of our garage roof just a couple of weeks ago. He is healing well as time progresses and it changed the whole way I think about life. I've always known that life can change in a minute, but that is the closest I've ever been to not knowing what the future would hold, as Mark lay on his back on the asphalt in a pool of blood. He was lucky that day and so was I. Life is too short to be taken for granted. This Thanksgiving, I am most grateful for our medical system and that time heals many things. I am also grateful for the return of the Monarchs that bring us silent messages, if we are open to them. The scientists are saying that this may be the best year ever in Mexico or at least the best in a very long time.

Now to get back to the purple dragonfly. Well, Mark had a very bruised derrière on the side where he hit the ground. As it healed, it changed colour and the markings did as well. One day I noticed he had a very unusual pattern developing... it looked like a purple dragonfly! The next day it looked even more like a dragonfly. Yes, I have a vivid imagination but to me it really did look like a dragonfly. I have tried to document these stories with photos, but some things are just better left to the imagination.

As I wait for my last chrysalis to eclose, probably today, I bid farewell not only to my final Monarch but also to the writing of this book. May the Monarchs continue to prosper and flood our world with Monarch Magic. I look forward to seeing them on their wondrous mountains in Mexico, in February.

*Author's Note (p.m.)

I wrote the ending to this book this morning while visiting Rachel. When I talked to Mark at home, he was pretty sure that our last chrysalis would be out tomorrow. It hadn't darkened up much yet.

When I returned home around 7:00 p.m. I went to take a look. Our final Monarch was hanging from its chrysalis shell so had probably come out just minutes before. Good timing I would say; in time for Thanksgiving and on the last day of writing this book. I am not surprised, even though they usually eclose in the morning. Now it needs to get on its way to Mexico!

Also by coincidence, my first book "When a Butterfly Speaks ... Whispered Life Lessons" was published today. I received a voicemail from the publisher that it had, but I didn't get a chance to listen to it until after I got home. I checked on Amazon and sure enough, it was there.

So my last Monarch was indeed perfectly timed! After the ending was written to book two (at least I thought so at the time) and before I discovered that my first book was published! It was here in time to help celebrate.

This final Monarch of the season became a very special gift for a woman who lives in Wales and was widowed a few years ago.

My friend Carys, and her brother, Michael with his fiancé, Paulina from Wales released this tagged butterfly joyfully in memory of Nia's husband, Cedric. Carys was able to share the experience by sending a video to Wales on Nia's birthday. A true gift of friendship from the heart! Who knows? Maybe this Monarch will end up in Wales instead of Mexico.

Out of curiosity, I Googled whether Monarchs have been seen in Wales. On the very rare occasion, they have. The earliest recorded sighting was by a young boy in Neath, South Wales in 1876.(www.ukbutterflies.co.uk)

There are no milkweed plants there, so it is hypothesized that they had migrated as an adult from either North America, Madeira, Portugal or the Canary Islands.

Who knows what tomorrow will bring. All I can say is this is a THANKSGIVING to remember and I am truly grateful.

Wishing you many butterfly blessings! May the Monarchs continue to grace our world in abundance and may you be touched by their magic.

*Author's Note: All Thanksgiving weekend I was under the illusion that I was finished this book. Saturday, Sunday and Monday went by and the writing appeared to have stopped. Tuesday morning came and I was back at it. The words circulating in my head were not going to go away until I wrote them down.

2

Some Things to Think About...
Mysticism in Particular

October 11, 2018

My dear friend and fellow nature-lover, Pauline Bokkers wrote this beautiful piece today. I just had to share it!

"These stories bring hope and peace and joy, and the world so needs this right now, as do the butterflies. I think the recovery story of the Monarch should be a gauge for our human condition. If we plant seeds of hope and encouragement and tend lovingly to the marginalized, we can effect change. The Monarchs are proof."

I chatted with my inspirational friend, Luc Picard, this evening. He had started to read "When a Butterfly Speaks... Whispered Life Lessons" and said it was "mystical". I looked up its definition at Luc's recommendation and I think he hit the nail on the head. I haven't been able to put a word to the way these stories have come to be; now I can.

Even today's date holds many 1's. (10/11/2018). The year adds up to 11 as well. Very mystical!

October 12, 2018

My editor and friend, sent me this today after finishing the first editing of this second book. Her subject line simply said, "Mystical". She obviously had read the previous paragraph that I had just added.

"Hi Barb,

I loved the second book as much as the first! After I finished, I got an email that I had a book credit. I was lead to purchase a book where mysticism was discussed.

The first example the author gives is walking in a forest and observing a butterfly feeding on a flower!

I agree that the books are mystical. Thank you for the honour of sharing these stories with me. Butterflies have an incredible way of changing our view of the world.

Blessings,

Angela"

Just minutes after I received Angela's email, my friend, Pauline used the word mystical to describe an event that occurred today in a text. Then my friend, Ev did too!

I now knew I was getting the message loud and clear. Not everything can or needs to be explained. That makes life interesting!

I love this quote from Dr. Wayne Dyer in his book "Ten Secrets to Success and Inner Peace".

"The ability to participate in true miracles— true miracles in your life— happens when you open your mind to your limitless potential."

I would add your heart to this quote as well; our mind and heart seem to be connected.

October 13, 2018

Again, thoughts were circulating in my head and I needed to get up and write them down before they were lost forever.

I was reminded that Lincoln Brower's actions, many years ago and right up until the end of his life, have had a tremendous influence on the Monarchs

Barbara J. Hacking

and their survival. Alongside others, his work was crucial in protecting the Monarchs overwintering habitat, especially from illegal logging. When we see a Monarch may we be reminded of his dedication to this beautiful insect.

May the wondrous nature of his work continue to ripple throughout the Monarchs' world, on into the future.

3

Ted's Birthday

October 18, 2018 (10/18/18)

Here we go again! This book doesn't want to end! I truly thought the writing would stop now that the Monarchs had left for Mexico. It appears that the numbers are speaking to me as I edit this book.

What started out as a day where snow blanketed the earth ended up being a gorgeous, sunny Autumn day. It was Ted Blowes' birthday. Today, my mentor would have been 82 years old.

Oh, how he is missed by his family and friends! His name still circulates at Communities in Bloom and Civic Beautification and Environmental Awareness Committee meetings. Projects that promote Ted's commitment to the environment and education are still being carried out. He was a pioneer in this area and created awareness wherever he went. He continues to live on in the memories of those who were lucky enough to have known him and the actions of those he mentored.

The Ted Blowes Memorial Pollinator Peace Garden has become a magical place. All the ideals that Ted held close to his heart radiate from this garden. Each season its purpose changes.

In the Spring, the tiny plants pop up out of the Earth, reminding us of rebirth and the world awakening once again. When the tiny Milkweed shoots pop up, we are reminded that the Monarchs will be here soon.

In the Summer, the flowers come alive as the pollinators dance among them, sipping their sweet nectar and bringing joy to those who visit. The Ice Ballet Milkweed flourishes, nourishing the Monarchs and their young. All the other pollinators love it too. They call out to us to protect their environment. They are gracing the land once again because of people like Ted who realized that they were in trouble; largely due to man's actions.

In the Autumn, the Milkweed seeds are gathered here and given to those who would love a piece of the garden and all it stands for. Once a seed is set in motion there is no telling where it will end up. It just rides the wind like a migrating Monarch until it lands at its new location. Each seed carries the new plant within, ready to spread the goodness. Children share in this magic as they blow the seeds into the air making wishes.

In the Winter, the garden rests along with all the pollinators hidden among it, awaiting the warmth of Spring as the Monarchs vacation in Mexico. The pollinator plants share their seeds with the birds who dare to stay and brave the elements.

This garden is a magical oasis indeed! It's a place to seek refuge from the busyness and stress of our world. Its constant transformation from one season to the next delights us, if we choose to engage. Even from one day to the next; no two days are ever alike in a garden. Today the sun shone down magnificently, setting the Autumn colours on fire.

I am truly grateful to Ted who had the foresight to create a place to help the pollinators. He will be remembered as an educator, an environmentalist and as a catalyst to make things happen.

It only seems right to try to end this book with more synchronicities I experienced on this day.

I had checked to see which birthday Ted would have been celebrating. He was born in 1936 so that makes it his 82nd. I was going off in my car this morning and these are the numbers on my dashboard.

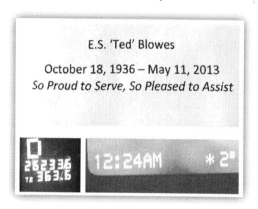

So many **36's!** Three 36's and another one backwards. The year that Ted was born! I also saw two 2's.

Then as I drove home it was 12:22 and 2 degrees C. So many twos. Unfortunately I couldn't stop in time to capture it in a photo. I did get a photo at 12:24 which at first I was disappointed with. It turns out to be 2 minutes after 12:22 which adds another 2 to the picture. (12:22+2) Look at the time 12:24. The first two numbers add up to 3 and the last two add up to 6. Put them together and what do you get? **36!**

*On June 30, 2019, while editing this book, I was showing my friend, Ruth the photo of my odometer that day. She noticed that the time 12:24 added up to **36** as well. (12+24=**36**) Even today's date 6/30 adds up to 36.

Now this is hard to believe but when I Googled 2 degrees C. to convert it for American readers, it was 35.6 degrees Fahrenheit! Now you can't get any closer to **36** than that!!! Oh my!!!

You can't make this stuff up! Why is it that these numbers want my attention? You must think that all I do is sit there, waiting for these patterns. I assure you this is not the case.

*Author's Note:

While editing this book, I discovered that adding up the numbers of the date when Ted passed on, created a 22.

(5+11+2+0+1+3= 22) That was on my odometer along with the 36's but I didn't put 2 and 2 together until much time had passed. No pun intended.

I was going off to Ted's garden, to plant red and white tulips that had been a gift at the National Communities in Bloom Symposium. Ted was one of the founders of this organization. The funny thing was that the bulbs had the words Gros Morne, Newfoundland on the package. Back in chapter 28, on a date adding up to **36**, I had found a wet piece of paper in Ted's Garden with "When a Butterfly Speaks" written on one side and Gros Morne, Newfoundland written on the other side. I hadn't published my book yet and had no connection to Gros Morne, until this very minute.

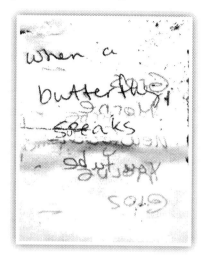

Ted used to say at our Communities in Bloom meetings, "Wouldn't it be lovely and patriotic if everyone in Stratford planted red and white flowers in their gardens." He thought that would just make Canada Day the best celebration ever! Last year, that happened throughout the country as we celebrated Canada's 150th year of Confederation. There were tulip bulbs that looked like Canadian flags, developed especially for this and part of a National Communities in Bloom 2017 Project. It was amazing to see them everywhere and Ted would have been in his glory.

Before I got in my car to go to Ted's garden, I went over to our pollinator garden beside the driveway. A little, yellowish bird startled me as it flew out from the lilac tree. At first I thought it was a butterfly, but logic told me it couldn't be with the cooler temperatures. It didn't stay long enough for me to pull out my camera.

When I got to the garden, I saw the exact same kind of bird. My friend Pauline, an avid birder identified it as a male Goldfinch, wearing its winter attire. Its bright, yellow summer feathers had faded so it would camouflage more readily in the naked trees.

It was eating seeds from the plants in Ted's garden. It flew to the skeletal remains of what was once a beautiful Ice Ballet Milkweed plant and just sat there looking at me. I'm sure he was telling me that gardens should be left in the Fall, so the birds will have seeds for the winter and places to perch. The birds will also help transplant those seeds to new places. This feathered friend was really enjoying Ted's garden and so was I.

Many pollinators winter over in dry leaves and in hollow stems, as well. Once the temperature is consistently above 50 degrees F. (10 degrees C.), a garden can be cleaned up without worrying about disturbing the pollinators. They will be enjoying the warmer weather, and you will be too.

I planted the bulbs and look forward to seeing them in the Spring, joining the Milkweed shoots when they pop out of the earth.

In honour of Ted's Birthday, 82 packages of milkweed seeds from his garden have been sent off to be shared with people in Toronto, Canada's first Bee City. Happy Birthday, Ted!

October 21, 2018

I awoke at 6:30 a.m. this morning. I really thought I was finished this book. Usually when I awaken early, I have words circulating in my head that I need to write down; today it was numbers.

If you look at Ted's Birthday date and add the year, it makes 36. His birth year. 18+18=36.

Or if you take the year, 2018 and multiply the 2 by the 18 you get 36.

Even the time I awoke this morning has a 3 and a 6 in it.

If you add the month and the date (10 + 18) you get 28. If you turn the numbers around, you get Ted's age. Wow! Even the year 2018 hides Ted's age.

It comes as no surprise to me that the meaning of 36 is moving away from materialism and shifting to a life of pure love and mysticism.

It also symbolizes humanitarianism and looking for creative ways to improve our world. These ideals perfectly describe Ted.

November 23, 2018

Today our Communities in Bloom Committee gathered for a photoshoot for our new Pollinator Pathway Project. So far, nine Pollinator trees have been planted to revitalize the land along the railway tracks. This will beautify the area, as well as give back valuable habitat to our native pollinators.

Can you see the big heart cloud behind us? I'm sure Ted was smiling from above. Perhaps they are angel wings.

As funding becomes available, this Pollinator Pathway will grow along two city blocks. It is important to find areas of land that we can repurpose for these valuable insects.

Barbara J. Hacking

December 10, 2018

Today I came across this quote, quite by accident, about the numbers 3, 6 and 9. (3 and 6 add up to 9)

> **"If you only knew the magnificence of 3, 6 and 9 then you would have the key to the universe."**
>
> **Nikola Tesla (1856-1943)**

Today's date 12/10/2018 adds up to 33 (12 +10+2+0+1+8). More 3's! Added together they make 6 and multiplied, make 9. Very strange indeed!

December 13, 2018 (12/13/2018)

I was thinking of Ted today as I watched the birds, using the plant stems like trampolines. Their rapid movement caught my attention as I sat at our kitchen table. They would fly to the surrounding trees and then jump down to the bendable branches. They were having so much fun frolicking in the sunshine, which doesn't come to visit as often this time of the year, and dining on the seeds. We really should leave our gardens alone until the spring. Less work in the fall and more work in those early days of spring when we are itching to get outside.

Today's date adds up to 36. (12+13+2+0+1+8) Coincidence? Maybe... or synchronicity, for those who have eyes to see it.

Looking back at the day this book started reveals another 36. (7/18/2018)

*Author's Note: I have been finding some interesting information about numbers from Olga at www.researchmaniacs.com and decided to check out 3636 and its meaning. She gives the letters D Q N H E J T as possible clues for a message. I immediately saw Ted's name as well as the first letter of eighty (E) and the first letter of two (T), Ted's age.

(http:/researchmaniacs.com/Numerology/Angel-Numbers/Angel-Numbers.html and http:/researchmaniacs.com/Astrology/Olga.html)

4

Finale?

October 20, 2018

You may recall from the very first chapter, that numbers began to appear that gave me a clear message it was time for my last book to come to its natural conclusion and move on to something new. Today I saw this taxi. It even moved in front of us from the other lane, as if to make sure I saw the numbers it adorned.

Lots of 8's and 9's... and my initials B. J.

Shortly thereafter, I saw a huge butterfly cloud in the sky, similar to when I ended my first book. Coincidences? Perhaps.

While editing I noticed that the four 9's make 36. If you have read Ending Number 3, you will know the significance of that.

5

Grand Finale?

October 31, 2018

Today is Halloween, here in Canada. I would like to try to end this book with a good laugh. The Skeletons of Vivian Line here in Stratford, Ontario enjoy sharing the fun of Halloween with others. Each day they embark on a new adventure and curious people come from far and wide to see what they are up to. Recently, the skeletons celebrated their 100th scene with no repeats. Herein lies imagination, at its best!

In this particular scene the skeletons are bug and butterfly catching.(@ skeletonsofvivianline)

Brains behind the Operation and Photo Credit: Melissa McKerlie

As the skeletons would say, "Remember to smile... laugh…and enjoy!" I think the butterflies would say the same thing... Life is too short to do otherwise.

I had awoken early this morning with words circulating in my head, once again. This book just doesn't seem to want to stop! I went back to catch a little more sleep and had the most vivid dream about a skeleton... of a plant.

I had found a potted milkweed that was just the skeletal remains of the original plant. It was covered with Monarch caterpillars trying to eat the leftover stems after the luscious leaves were all eaten. Of course, I was developing a plan to rescue them. What was I going to feed them? The Milkweed was all dried up. Then I woke up realizing that the Monarchs had gone. My panic subsided.

*Editor's Note

Here it is a year later. As I was waiting to publish this book, I was compelled to add this photo. It has absolutely nothing to do with butterflies but I'm sure if they truly could speak, they would bring us the same message.

Photo Credit: Melissa McKerlie
The Skeletons of Vivian Line

6

Monarchs in Mexico/Pumpkins Here

November 1, 2018 (11/1/2018)

Today is Dia de Los Muertos (Day of the Dead), where the Mexican people will celebrate the lives of their loved ones who have passed on. This celebration developed because the people would see the Monarchs flying above them in great numbers on their way to the mountain tops and believed they were the spirits of their dearly departed family members, returning to them for a visit. After a wonderful Monarch season here, I can imagine it will be one of the best celebrations in a long time. The Monarchs are now in their capable hands, until next Spring.

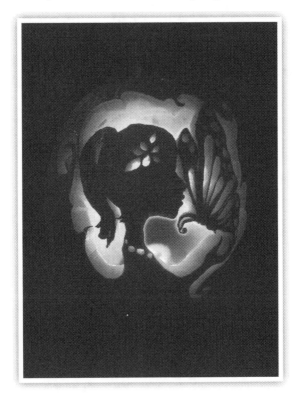

As the Mexicans celebrate The Day of the Dead, Stratford, Ontario, Canada celebrates with their annual Pumpkin Parade. People from all over the city give their Jack-o-lanterns a chance to shine once again. They bring them to the town square the day after Halloween and they are lit once more for all to enjoy. At the end of the night they are thrown into huge trucks and off they go to be fed to wild boars. This keeps many pumpkins out of the landfill. My favourite pumpkin this year was this beauty.

My friend Carys, happened to overhear the most touching conversation between a young girl and her Mother, which really touched her heart. As the little girl ran her fingers over the beautiful carving, she identified the wings and the antennae eagerly and a huge smile lit up her face. You see, this little girl was blind. Butterflies are delightful in many ways.

Even when they are no longer here, butterflies show up in interesting ways and can make one smile.

7

Update from Mexico and California

December 10, 2018

People in Mexico are ecstatically reporting that there are more Monarchs this year than they have seen in a long time!

The Monarchs arrived later than expected. Their migration was apparently slowed down by cooler temperatures in Texas. The spectacular entrance was well worth the wait!

I am grateful for the daily reports and videos on social media that bring the Monarchs back to us, while we miss their physical presence.

I marvel at how they never collide when flying; even when you can hardly see through the kaleidoscope of orange they are creating.

On one hand, perhaps humanity is doing something right, as the numbers of Monarchs skyrocket in Mexico to levels not seen in many years. On the other hand, the reports from California are not so glorious. They are seeing very few there. The Xerces Society who does a yearly count of this population is saying that the Californian Monarch population is down 86 percent since the previous year and over 99% down from what it was. Why is this so? Reasons such as drought and forest fires have been given. Also the use of herbicides and pesticides, lack of milkweed, logging, urban development and climate change are all possible causes. Perhaps they have simply decided to go to Mexico? Perhaps they were an isolated population from centuries past?

Man must continue to listen to the messages the Monarchs bring to us. We must respect and take care of Mother Earth, and be truly grateful for the planet we have the privilege of sharing with these magnificent creatures and all the other animals.

May we never forget what we once lost or may lose, if we aren't careful.

January 31, 2019

Yesterday the World Wildlife Fund Mexico announced the numbers for the Monarch overwintering grounds in Mexico. According to them, the Monarch population is up 144 % since last year and the best year recorded since the 2006-2007 season. That is wonderful news!

I must admit I still thought it would be much higher. Mark and I have only seen a year like this one (2018), once in the last 35 years. I still think that counting Monarchs is next to impossible.

Experts are cautioning that the weather conditions this year were perfect for Monarchs but that could change. They are warning us that the Eastern Monarchs are still not out of the woods and we shouldn't develop a false sense of security. The Western Monarch population has had a serious decline in number and that is extremely worrisome. Only time will tell what the future holds.

*

Fourteen years ago today, my dear father passed away. Two years ago, I won that journal that mystically started to fill up with Monarch stories. Today, I complete what I think could be the final editing of this book. Usually the official count isn't announced until March, so I am grateful for its early arrival to make it in, just under the wire.

February 14, 2019

Today, a new colony of Monarch butterflies was announced near the extinct Nevado de Toluca volcano.

In the nearby Mexican mountains, a colony was discovered in the area known as the Amanalco de Becerra Sanctuary.

Local landowners discovered that rumours that a new colony existed here were true, just before Christmas and the new colony's existence was verified by officials in mid-January. For years, they searched but were unsuccessful, until now. The larger numbers this year made the discovery possible.

This area is perfect for the Monarchs in terms of climate, water and nectar flowers and will NOT be open to the public. One has to wonder whether or not, the human footprint at the other sanctuaries affects the Monarchs in any way.

This new colony is welcomed news and certainly affects the accuracy of the number of Monarchs counted. Are there other colonies that have eluded mankind that are not included in the numbers? Monarchs like the tops of mountains and the summits are not always easily accessible.

Even with all the technology that has been developed, Monarchs remain a mystery in many ways.

8

The Real Ending! Finally!

December 22, 2018

I have been editing this book and although I have tried to end it many times, as you can see, it seems fitting to end it today. When I looked at the clock just before going to bed, this is what I saw.

The date and the time matched. When I checked the meaning of 1222, it was encouraging me to move in a different direction; so I am. Happily, gracefully and gratefully.

All of a sudden it dawned on me that the writing of these two books started on the anniversary of my Father's death, January 31, 2017 and ends today on the 9th anniversary of my Mother's death. Exactly 22 months and 22 days of writing. Even today's date has four 2's in a row (12/22/2018). I couldn't have planned that, even if I had tried! Very mystical!

These are the numbers I saw when I finally ended "When a Butterfly Speaks… Whispered Life Lessons". Interestingly, 2222 means "now is a perfect time to work on your ability to let go".(www.spitualunite.com) It is also a reminder that divine guidance is present. (Numerologist.com) So it's all beginning to make sense. Both messages were well received.

Curiously, I checked to see how long it took to write the first book and it was 17 months and 17 days. That means this one took 5 months and 5 days. Why is it that I am not surprised?

Thanks Mom and Dad, for all that you were and all that you are. Whether it's through memories or whether you are still with me, matters not. How lucky I was to have had you for parents! Your presence is felt often and in many ways. Your wise words still linger.

I am almost sure this time, that this book is finished! When I went out to my car, I saw this.

5525 twice! According to Olga, (http:/researchmaniacs.com/Numerology/Angel-Numbers/Angel-Numbers.html and http:/researchmaniacs.com/Astrology/Olga.html) 5525 is associated with the letters D, A, J, V, Q, K and

E. She suggests rearranging these letters to get a message or meaningful initials.

I can see DAD, D. E. for my mother Dorothy Eccles, A. J. E. which are the initials of my Grandpa, Adam James Eccles who enjoyed writing poetry and tended the most beautiful garden of raspberries and peas, and Ed is the short form for Edward which is Ted's real name. Four of the most influential people in my life who have passed on are perhaps still guiding me. (All of this from only 4 of the 7 letters) Are they the masterminds behind these two books?

The image number for the above photo was 2005, which has another 25 within it. My Mother's birthday was January 25 and the year my Dad passed away was 2005. Uncanny.

When looking at the 5525 on both of the odometers, I see 5 X 5 =25; my Mom's birthday number, once again. Even her birth date adds up to 25. (1+2+5+1+9+1+6=25)

The 26 at the beginning of the odometer is my Mother's birth date in disguise. January 25th translates to 1 + 25 = 26.

I realized that 25 seems to be my Mom's Number. Ted's number is 36. My Dad was born on November 14, 1914 so it makes sense that his number is 14. Next month it will be the 14th anniversary of his death. It is interesting that when you put these three special numbers in order (14 25 36) there is an ascending numerical pattern and it goes up by 11's.

The day after making this discovery I woke up at 5:27. These numbers add to 14 and 25 is hidden within it. If you multiply the first and last number and add the middle one you get 37. My parents' address began with a 37 and they lived there for over 60 years.

A few days later I drove in the driveway after my Yoga class. There was a bright light shining on the time of 11:22 and the temperature of 14 degrees C. Investigating further, the temperature is my Dad's number. When you add the 11 to it you get my Mom's number of 25 and when you add the 22 to my Dad's number you get Ted's number. Very mystical indeed. What's more mystical is that I noticed this at all. Perhaps it was seeing the 11:12 and 13 degrees on the dashboard just minutes before while I was driving. Even that added up to 36.)

While I was editing, my cousin Bonnie kindly sent me this photo, quite out of the blue. It has my Mom (center), my Dad (top left) and I'm in the arms of my Grandpa Eccles. It would have been taken 55 years ago!! (5x5=25)

It was sent to her from another cousin, in the United States and it's funny how it would find its way to me in Canada at exactly the right time, as I wrote this ending. Very interesting!

This is probably the only photo that ever existed that includes my parents, my grandparents and I.

Also, when editing, I noticed the J for January and the D for December among the letters; the months when my parents transitioned into the next realm. The month when book one started, and the month when the second book ended.

Apparently, 5525 also means changes are ahead and at last, freedom will be experienced. (www.sunsigns.org) After 22 months and 22 days of writing, it will be nice to enjoy the holiday season and just relax, although I have loved every minute of writing.

This ending is certainly the best Christmas present ever! The universe works in mysterious ways and I am eternally grateful!

I realized that this book is just a continuation of the first and the final title was decided; "When a Butterfly Speaks... The Sequel... Celebrating the Return of the Silent Messengers".

> **"Eventually all the pieces fall into place. Until then, laugh at the confusion, live for the moment, and know that EVERYTHING HAPPENS FOR A REASON."**

> **Albert Schweitzer (1875-1965)**

I think all the pieces have fallen into place. All I could do was laugh when I wasn't sure what was going on... and I'm still not sure, so I'll just keep on laughing. I will move on into the future, not dwelling on what was, but what is. With time, I'm sure the reasons will become clear.

Little did I know that this book would contain so many coincidences regarding numbers when I first began to write it. I couldn't have planned them, even if I had tried.

Right after I wrote the previous sentence, I came across the Course of Miracles' Lesson 135, 11 and 12. I was just going through my emails and again funnily, it showed up at exactly the right time! (Lesson 135 = 1+35 =36)

> **"A healed mind does not plan. It carries out the plans that it receives through listening to wisdom that is not its own. It waits until it has been taught what should be**

313

done, and then proceeds to do it. It does not depend upon itself for anything except its adequacy to fulfill the plans assigned to it. It is secure in certainty that obstacles can not impede its progress to accomplishment of any goal that serves the greater plan established for the good of everyone.

A healed mind is relieved of the belief that it must plan, although it cannot know the outcome which is best, the means by which it is achieved, nor how to recognize the problem that the plan is made to solve."

These two books have been an exercise of surrendering, trusting and having faith that I was doing what I was meant to do. There certainly have been many surprises along the way. It is now time to let go... at least for now.

Wishing you many butterfly hugs as you let go of what no longer serves you.

May your butterfly blessings be many!

Barb

Author's Final Notes

January 31, 2019

I had moved on to a new journal but was directed to interweave what I had written into this book, so the never-ending book continues. I had a wee break at Thanksgiving and then again, at Christmas. As I have been editing, the messages have not stopped.

It is minus 24 degrees Celsius outside and the last few days have been perfect for hibernating and doing an additional edit of this book. I honestly believed that I was done!

Today is also the 14th anniversary of my dear Dad's passing. Even the date creates his number 14. (1 and 3+1) I simply must add what happened.

Exactly two years ago, I won the journal that began to magically fill with stories, with me holding the pen. Today was no less mystical.

I asked for a sign that my Dad was still with me, and I was not disappointed.

While having dinner, Mark noticed a bright red Cardinal in the naked tree right outside the kitchen window. The setting sun acted like a spotlight on him. He was just sitting there patiently waiting for us, his chosen audience, to notice him shining on this wintry stage. It was frigidly cold; an evening not fit for man or beast. As soon as he was sure we had seen him, he flew off. (Thanks, Dad!!)

I'm not surprised that a Cardinal was my Dad's chosen way of getting our attention. On the day of his death, my brothers and I witnessed a beautiful cardinal singing away, in the tree across the road from my parents' house as we arrived to make funeral arrangements. He was singing at the top of his lungs, making sure we did not pass him by. His bright red coat was cheerful, his song was music to our ears and we certainly appreciated the visit. Was this a coincidence?

That day, I had secretly wished for my Dad to send me a butterfly but I knew that was impossible on January 31st, in Canada... Or was it?

As I drove home along the country roads watching the sun set, it transformed into a magnificent butterfly shape bearing the magical Monarch colours of orange and black. It was as if time stood still and it was just the sunset and I.

I had received my sign and that moment will be embedded in my memory's camera forever. I believe it was the first sign I had ever received from what I perceived to be, the other side. I'm glad it wasn't the last.

This special memory began my first book and now ends the second.

When releasing butterflies I have seen many special signs. Clouds morphing into hearts, butterflies and other shapes. Feathers falling from the sky. Up until now I simply wrote about my observations. Were they coincidences or divinely guided signs? How does one prove it?

I now believe we aren't meant to, but need faith that each sign is special and carries a message from beyond this world. In order to have faith one must believe in what can't be seen.

My dear Mother used to have a mustard seed embedded in a glass bubble, that she often wore as a brooch. It reminded her of the Bible's teaching that it was better to have faith the size of a mustard seed than no faith at all; also, that even a little bit of faith could do a lot.

I guess I never really thought about what this meant, until now. My daughter still has that mustard seed, kept as a cherished memory of her Grandmother (Thanks Mom!!).

So these two books began and ended on January 31st. I wonder if the mystical experiences will stop now that they are finished? We will have to wait and see.

What's the next best thing to receiving a butterfly from my Dad, in wintry weather?..... Serenity finding a Swallowtail butterfly chrysalis in a haystack. This is virtually next to impossible when you see how camouflaged the chrysalis would be against the colour of the hay. Serenity has a great eye for finding butterflies; even on the final day of January. It truly is like finding a needle in a haystack.

It's also like receiving a raincheck to receive a butterfly at a later date, when it's safe for it to come out. I predict it will come out on Father's Day. Until then, it awaits with our other Swallowtail chrysalids.

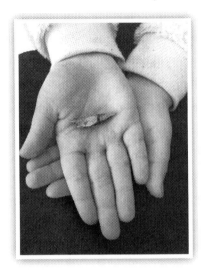

Are the Monarchs going to continue to speak to me? I have a feeling that they are.

Are the numbers going to stop?... I have a feeling they are not.

318

February 6, 2019

Today while meditating, I was directed back to these numbers that appeared on my dashboard as this book came to an end. Taking a closer look, I saw six 6's. Add them together... and voila! 36! The image number for this photo in the book has a 36 and the time numbers multiplied (9x4), also equals 36. There is even a 36 hidden among the numbers. The date Ted passed away added up to 22 and it is there too. (Thanks Ted!!)

I guess that answers one of my questions!

I just looked at the clock and it's 11:11.

February 11, 2019 (2/11/2019)

This morning I finished another edit of this book. I won't call it the final edit because this book doesn't seem to want to come to an end.

Mark and I were driving to Cambridge, our hometown, and we saw the time 11:11 and smiled. It also creates today's date if you add the first two 1's together.

Shortly thereafter, I was walking around downtown and was greeted with this on the wet sidewalk. I couldn't believe my eyes! Monarchs always have an interesting way of appearing in my life; even in the Winter. I think they are telling me I'm finished, as well. Look at the time!

11:44 means new beginnings. Every time I saw the time today, there were reminders.

According to Olga (http:/researchmaniacs.com/Numerology/Angel-Numbers/Angel-Numbers.html and http:/researchmaniacs.com/Astrology/Olga.html), the following letters contain a message relating to 1144.

M E C S W K N

The first message that popped out at me was "ME". Yes, I need to look after my own self care. Perhaps it is ME that has poured out my soul in these books. I absolutely, positively know I have had guidance, but I am beginning to entertain the thought that my soul may have been whispering to me, as well.

More importantly, I need to spend more time with **M**ark **E**dward, my dear husband. Spring is coming so I look forward to our time hiking in nature and finding new places to explore. He has been amazingly supportive throughout the writing of these books. When the words came in the middle of the night or while we were in the car, he patiently just let me do what I needed to do and I am eternally grateful.

Intermingled among the letters are the initials of many of my friends. I look forward to spending more time with them, as well as my children.

The letter M reminds me of the Magical Monarch Mountains in Macheros, Mexico and also in the State of Michoacán. When you look at all the letters together you can almost see the word "Mexican".

In 12 days, I will be there celebrating the return of these silent messengers. I look forward to exchanging the flurries of snow here in Canada, for the flurries of Monarchs dancing around us. It truly is the most magical place on Earth and with the magnificent number of Monarchs this year, I can hardly wait for the incredible show to begin.

So these two books have taken 2 years and 11 days to write. Look at today's date. (2/11)

I guess I was waiting for a message from the butterflies to know I was truly done; and that answers my other question.

February 14, 2019.

Now this is becoming embarrassing. This really is a never-ending book. Again! I tried to start a third book but I keep getting directed back to this one.

Today I saw the numbers 2727, on my trip odometer. The regular odometer has 27 hidden in it twice, one forward and one backwards. When I checked it's meaning, I was given the following letters to decipher as to what these numbers meant. (http:/researchmaniacs.com/Numerology/Angel-Numbers/ Angel-Numbers.html and http:/researchmaniacs.com/Astrology/Olga.html)

I L M B V K and T

These letters were very interesting coming up on Valentine's Day, especially the V.

I see I, L for I Love.
M for Mark, Monarchs, Mexico, Magical, Mountains, Macheros, Michoacán.
B for Barb, Butterflies, Books, Bears.
K for Kisses and Kindness on Valentine's Day; also my Kids.
I don't see an E for ending this book.
I guess the T could stand for terminate (or The End).

2727 also means good news is on its way and to be open to the signs and synchronicities.

The 27th is the date of my first official date with Mark, our wedding anniversary, our daughter, Rachel's birthday and our son, Ryan's age.

When you add 2+7+2+7, you get 18 which is Ted's birthday. Multiplying the 2 and the 7 you get 14 which is my Dad's number. If you take the 27 and subtract the 2, you get my Mom's number, 25.

My good and wise friend, Kimberley Sunshine Parry recently said that she had a feeling that letters of the alphabet were going to start giving me messages, as well as numbers. Perhaps she was right.

February 14 is the approximate date when Monarchs in Mexico begin to reproduce to create the generation that will begin the Northward migration. This date brings hope that the huge number of Monarchs in Mexico will multiply like crazy, so that the Summer of 2019 will be even more spectacular.

February 15, 2019

I awoke at 6:54. Descending numbers have directed me back in time before and this was no exception.

For some reason, a poem I received from a teacher who first climbed the Monarch mountains with me, back in 2005 came to mind. I jumped out of bed and quickly found the printed email she sent with the poem. It was dated March 24 (3/24) which adds up to 27. Even today's date adds up to 27 (2/15/19 = 2+15+1+9=27).

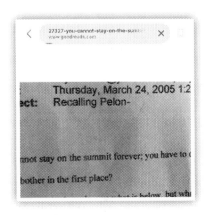

When I Googled the poem, this number caught my attention at the top of the screen, as I waited for the poem to load. (27327) I think I was getting the message to include it in this book. Is this the ending I've been waiting for?

> "You cannot stay on the summit forever; you have to come down again.
> So why bother in the first place?...
>
> By Rene Daumal

I believe I could write a new version.

You can not keep writing this book forever,
you have to stop sometime.
Is it now?
Time will tell.

February 22, 2019 (2/22/2019) (2+22+2+0+1+9=36).

This book played like a movie before me, as I slept. When I awoke from this vivid dream and looked at the clock, it read 2:22. I smiled and knew at that moment that this book was complete. 2 years and 22 days of writing. Even today's date mirrors those numbers. Adding the numbers in the date, is 36. (Ted's number that always seems to show up at amazing times.)

There are already reports from Journey North that the Monarchs are beginning their migration north to Texas, where the females will present the next generation. It will be the Monarchs that emerge from these eggs that will continue the amazing journey, northward. This is almost a full month earlier than normal, so hopefully the weather, the wind and the growth of milkweed will be kind to them. Will they be the Monarchs that create new stories for a third book?

The next time I looked at the clock it was 4:56. Those ascending numbers remind me that I'm only a day away from climbing the stairway to heaven.

Tomorrow I will be standing on one of the mountains, with the Monarchs. Life can't get any better than that!

There are no endings, just great beginnings.

Photo Credit: Luc Picard (Center photo)
Photo credit: (Top right) Rachel Hacking

March 3, 2019

Here it is the third day of the third month. The year 2019 adds up to 12 and when you add those two numbers together you also get 3 (3/3/3).

Having just returned from the magical, Monarch mountains in Macheros last night, I end this book with the beginning of book number 3. Today, being on an all time nature high, after spending a week in the glorious winter home of the Monarchs, I am refreshed, recharged and ready to continue writing.

I have tried to start book 3 many times over the past few months but today feels perfect, and the numbers seem to be aligned. So the title has changed once again to "When a Butterfly Speaks 2... Celebrating the Return of the Silent Messengers".

"Celebrate endings-for they precede new beginnings."

Jonathan Lockwood Huie

Be sure to be on the lookout for "When a Butterfly Speaks 3... Connections Beyond Coincidence". Perhaps the purple dragonfly will pay a visit. Time will tell.

Our future lies in our imagination. Make it a good one!

*****

Take Care of the World... and the World will take Care of You!

Printed in the United States
By Bookmasters